THE BOOK OF

FISH
& SHELLFISH

THE BOOK OF

FISH
& SHELLFISH

HILAIRE WALDEN

Photographed by
JON STEWART

HPBooks

ANOTHER BEST SELLING VOLUME FROM HPBOOKS

HP Books
Published by the Berkley Publishing Group
A division of Penguin Putnam Inc.
375 Hudson Street
New York, NY 10014

9 8 7 6 5 4

ISBN: 1-55788-188-X

By arrangement with Salamander Books Ltd.
© Salamander Books Ltd. 1994, 2001

A member of the Chrysalis Group plc

The Penguin Putnam Inc. World Wide Web site address is:
http://www.penguinputnam.com

Home Economist: Kerenza Harries
Printed and bound in Spain

CONTENTS

INTRODUCTION

Fish and seafood are very much food of the nineties, the epitome of modern cooking and eating styles – low in fat, high in protein, rich in minerals and vitamins, quick and easy to prepare and cook, and versatile enough to be adapted to suit any occasion. Plus, many fish are cheaper than meat and better value for money.

The Book of Fish & Shellfish provides a varied, eclectic selection of more than 100 imaginative, attainable, and attractive recipes for today's cooks. Many different types of fish are included, from flounder and whiting, to tuna and mahi mahi, to mussels, lobster, and oysters; suitable alternatives are given where appropriate. The dishes use a wide variety of cooking methods, including steaming, poaching, cooking in parchment paper, braising, baking, and broiling and grilling.

There is a blend of new recipes and delicious versions of traditional favorites from around the world to cater for all tastes, budgets, and types of meals. These include Kedgeree for breakfast or brunch, to Hot Fish Loaf for a family lunch, to Lobster with Basil Dressing for special occasions, or Fish Cakes for a quick snack. Recipes are grouped according to the type of fish, such as flatfish, oily fish, and so on.

The book starts with a helpful section on buying, storing, preparing, and cooking fish. Techniques that are used frequently, such as filleting whole fish or cleaning mussels, are illustrated with step-by-step pictures.

PREPARING AND COOKING FISH

Fish and seafood are valuable in a balanced diet as they contain more natural goodness, weight for weight, than any other type of food. They are high in good-quality protein but low in calories.

All fish are rich stores of essential minerals and vitamins; fatty fish, such as herrings, mackerel, tuna, sardines, and salmon, are particularly good sources of vitamins A and D. They are also very easy to digest.

CHOOSING FISH

Really fresh fish is easy to recognize as it looks bright and fresh with vivid markings. The eyes are clear, bright, and slightly protruding, and the gills are pinkish or bright red (brown gills are a sure sign the fish is stale). Skin is firm and bright with bright scales that adhere tightly. The flesh is firm and elastic and springs back when pressed. Any smell is fresh and clean with just a hint of the sea: exceptions are shark and skate, which give off a natural smell of ammonia, which disappears on cooking.

Fillets and steaks should feel firm. The cut surfaces look translucent rather than opaque, and they should not be dry or shriveled. Avoid any that look slimy or have brown or yellow patches at the edges. If packaged, there should be no milky liquid.

A lot of the fish sold in supermarkets, and some fish markets, is thawed frozen fish. This has an unfortunate toll on its quality and limits its life. Thawed frozen fish should not be re-frozen.

Smoked fish should smell pleasant and smoky with no acid or musty odors. The flesh should be glossy and free from blemishes, and the color even. There should be no salt crystals, black soot, or blood marks.

PREPARING FISH

The recipes in this book assume that fish has been cleaned and scaled; a fishmonger will do this for you if it has not already been done. Skinning round fish presents no problems, but skinning flatfish, such as flounder, is more difficult and you may prefer to get your fishmonger to do it for you.

Filleting is quick and easy after a little practice and if you use the proper knife. A filleting knife has a flexible, pointed, straight-edged blade about 6 inches long. With this type of knife you can feel around soft fish bones, removing every last scrap of flesh from them. A really sharp edge to the blade is vital for skinning, boning, or filleting fish quickly, easily, and efficiently. However, fish skin will blunt the edge of the knife quickly, so the edge will need frequent sharpening.

You will also need a heavy knife for removing fish heads, kitchen scissors for snipping away the fins, a large board, and at least one clean, damp cloth.

Handle skinned and filleted fish with care and cook as soon as possible. Keep all the bones and trimmings for making stock.

COOKING FISH

Fish and seafood should be kept cool in between purchase and cooking, and should be cooked on the day of purchase. Fish and seafood respond well to all the healthy methods of cooking – steaming, poaching, baking, braising, and broiling or grilling.

Fish cooks quickly, but the flesh can dry out easily during cooking, becoming tough and disintegrating, especially when cooked by a dry method such as frying and broiling. To prevent this, fish should be basted frequently with oil, butter, or marinade during cooking, or protected by a coating, such as yogurt, bread crumbs, egg, or oatmeal.

When poaching fish, the liquid should remain at a very gentle bubble. Steaming is the most gentle method of cooking fish..

Choose the cooking method appropriate to the type and cut of fish. Delicate flatfish, and especially their fillets, need gentle cooking. Steaks of firm, fatty fish, or sturdy whole fish, can withstand cooking methods, such as grilling.

The general guideline for whole fish or pieces of fish more than 1 inch thick, is to allow 10 minutes for every 1 inch of flesh measured at its thickest point. When poaching, begin timing the moment the liquid starts to bubble gently.

Acid ingredients such as vinegar, citrus juice, or wine cook fish, so if fish is marinated in a mixture that contains one of these ingredients, it will take less time to cook by heat; the longer the marinating time, the shorter the cooking time.

When fish is cooked the flesh flakes when tested with the point of a sharp knife and will have just turned opaque. Flesh of fish on the bone will come away from the bone. To test tuna and swordfish, press the flesh – it will feel firm when cooked.

SUBSTITUTIONS
As fish and seafood are regional and seasonal, it is not always possible to buy the type specified in a recipe, but it is often possible to find a substitute, especially when fillets or steaks are called for. On the right are some examples of possible substitutes.

Sole/brill/flounder

Brill/turbot/John Dory

Porgy/scup/red bream

Cod/haddock/halibut/hake/monkfish

Red snapper/grouper/mahi mahi
(dolphin fish)

Pompano/pomfret/red snapper

Tuna/swordfish

Mackerel/herring

Bass/salmon, especially steaks
and fillets

Mussels/clams

SKINNING & FILLETING

SKINNING FLATFISH

Flatfish are usually skinned before filleting. Lay fish with its dark side up and head away from you. Make an incision in skin across bone where tail joins the body. Working from the cut, loosen a flap of skin with a thumbnail or knife. Hold tail firmly with one hand (a little salt on the fingertips or a cloth will help to get a firm grip) and pull skin sharply backward toward the head, not up. When you have removed skin as far as jaws, turn fish over and, holding it by the head, pull the skin until tail is reached.

FILLETING FLATFISH

Place fish with head away from you and eyes facing up. With point of knife, slit along length of backbone, from head to tail. Insert blade of knife between flesh and ribs to one side of backbone, next to head. With short, slicing movements, keeping blade next to ribs and at a shallow angle, separate flesh from bones. Continue working along length of ribs, following contours of fish's shape, until tail is reached. Cut fillet off at tail and trim. Remove other fillet on top of bone, turn fish over, and repeat with underside.

FILLETING ROUND FISH

These are usually skinned after filleting: you will get 2 fillets from a round fish. Place fish on its side. Place point of knife beside dorsal fin, then cut down along backbone to tail, keeping blade just above center of backbone, but close to upper bones of rib cage. Cut from dorsal fin to head end. Raise top fillet slightly. Working from head to tail, work fillet away from ribs with a slicing motion of blade. Slice along backbone again, this time with knife placed just below center. Lift away backbone and ribs.

SKINNING FILLETS

Lay the fillet skin side down on the work surface and make an incision through the flesh across the tail end. With the knife blade, loosen about 1/2 inch of flesh. Grip the skin at the tail end (a little salt on the fingertips or a cloth will help to grip firmly), slant the knife away from you, and work toward head, slicing through flesh, very close to the skin, and pushing the flesh away with knife.

PREPARING SHELLFISH

CLEANING MUSSELS
Wash mussel shells, scrape off any barnacles, and cut off fibrous beards protruding from where shells join; discard any cracked mussels or those that do not close when tapped. Scrub mussels under cold running water.

SHELLING SHRIMP
To shell shrimp, pull the head from body, then peel shell from body, leaving tail tip on if liked. For jumbo shrimp, make a shallow cut along back and remove dark intestinal thread running along it.

OPENING SCALLOPS
Give any shells that are open a sharp tap; if they remain open, discard them. Protect your hand with a cloth (and strong rubber gloves for added protection, if wished), then place scallop, flat side up, in palm. Insert point of a strong, short-bladed knife between shells near hinge and at 45 degree angle to it. (You may need to push and twist a little before it goes in.) Twist knife until the shell opens slightly.

Slide a finger between shells, then, with the knife in other hand, quickly and carefully cut around top shell to free the muscle and allow shells to be opened completely. Push the top shell backward to snap hinge. Using a small, sharp knife, carefully remove the grayish outer fringe of scallop; do not damage flesh. Slide the knife point under black threads on the side of the scallop, then gently pull it and the attached intestinal bag away. Ease the scallop from shell and rinse under cold running water.

— BRILL WITH CARDAMOM —

4 brill or sole fillets, about 6 ounces each
Generous 1 cup fish stock
2 teaspoons cornstarch
Juice of 1 large lemon
Seeds from 4 or 5 cardamom pods, toasted and ground
2 egg yolks
3 tablespoons unsalted butter, diced
Salt and pepper
Lemon wedges to garnish
Tomato, orange, and green onion salad to serve

Preheat oven to 350F (175C). Fold fillets in half, then place in a single layer in a baking dish.

Pour stock over fish. Cover and cook in the oven about 18 minutes or until just cooked through. Transfer fish to warm plates, season, cover, and keep warm. Meanwhile, in a bowl, mix together cornstarch, lemon juice, ground cardamom seeds, and egg yolks.

Stir a little fish cooking liquid into cornstarch mixture. Into a nonstick saucepan, pour remaining liquid, then stir in cornstarch mixture. Heat gently, stirring, until sauce thickens. Remove from heat and gradually stir in butter. Season with salt and pepper. Pour sauce around or over fish, garnish with lemon wedges, and serve with salad.

Makes 4 servings.

- STEAMED BRILL & VEGETABLES -

2 leeks, cut into fine strips
2 zucchini, cut into fine strips
2 stalks celery, cut into fine strips
3 green onions, thinly sliced
2 sprigs thyme
3 sprigs parsley
1 small sprig rosemary
Salt and pepper
2 tablespoons lemon juice
4 brill or sole fillets
2 tablespoons olive oil

Bring a saucepan of salted water to a boil. Add leeks, zucchini, celery, and green onions.

Boil vegetables 1 minute, then drain and refresh under cold running water. Lay vegetables in bottom of a steaming basket. Add thyme, parsley, and rosemary and sprinkle with salt and pepper.

Pour lemon juice over fillets, then fold them over and place on top of vegetables. Add water to a saucepan. Bring to a boil. Place steaming basket on top and steam about 4 minutes. Discard herbs, season fish, and drizzle olive oil over them. Serve fish with vegetables.

Makes 4 servings.

Note: Garnish with fresh sprigs of herbs, if wished.

- SOLE WITH MINT & CUCUMBER -

Cucumber, halved lengthwise, seeded, and cut into
   2-inch strips
Salt and white pepper
4 sole fillets, 6 to 7 ounces each, skinned
1 small shallot, finely chopped
3/4 cup fish stock
1/2 cup medium-dry white wine
3/4 cup crème fraîche or sour cream
5 mint leaves, torn
2 tablespoons unsalted butter, diced
Mint leaves to garnish
Snow peas to serve

Into a colander, place cucumber. Sprinkle
with salt and let drain 30 minutes. Rinse and
dry well with paper towels. Fold fillets in half,
skinned side in. Into a skillet, place folded
fillets with shallot. Add stock and wine and
heat until just simmering. Poach 4 to 5
minutes, then transfer to a warm plate and
cover to keep warm.

Add cucumber to poaching liquid, increase
heat, and boil until liquid is reduced by three-
quarters. Add crème fraîche or sour cream
and boil until beginning to thicken. Add
mint, salt, pepper, and juices collected on
plate with fish. Simmer 3 minutes. Remove
pan from heat and gradually swirl in butter.
Spoon sauce over fish. Serve garnished with
mint leaves, accompanied by snow peas.

Makes 4 servings.

——SOLE WITH CHIVE SAUCE——

1/2 cup cottage cheese, drained and pressed through a
    fine strainer
Grated peel and juice of 1 lemon
Salt and pepper
3-1/2 ounces cooked shelled shrimp, finely chopped
8 sole or flounder fillets, skinned
1 cup fish stock
1 small shallot, finely chopped
1 tablespoon dry white vermouth
6 tablespoons dry white wine
3/4 cup whipping cream, fromage frais, or cream cheese
1-1/2 tablespoons finely snipped fresh chives
Shrimp and snipped fresh chives to garnish
Broccoli to serve

Preheat oven to 350F (175C). Grease a shallow baking dish. In a bowl, beat together cottage cheese and lemon peel and juice. Season with salt and pepper. Stir in shrimp. Spread mixture on skinned side of fillets, then roll up neatly. Secure with wooden picks. Place fish in a single layer in dish, pour in stock to come halfway up the rolls, and add chopped shallot. Cover dish and cook in the oven about 20 minutes or until fish begins to flake. Meanwhile, in a small saucepan, boil vermouth and wine until reduced by half.

Transfer fillets to a warm plate and keep warm. Add stock and shallot to wines and boil until reduced by three-quarters. Stir in cream, if using, and simmer to a light creamy consistency. If using fromage frais or cream cheese, stir in and heat without boiling. Quickly pour sauce into a blender and mix until frothy. Add chives and seasoning. Pour some sauce over fish and serve rest separately. Garnish fillets with shrimp and chives and serve with broccoli.

Makes 4 servings.

— SOLE WITH LETTUCE FILLING —

4 sole fillets
Salt and pepper
Squeeze of lemon juice
1 tablespoon medium-dry white wine
1 tablespoon finely chopped white part of leek
1-1/2 cups finely shredded Iceberg lettuce
6 tablespoons ricotta cheese, pressed through a fine
    strainer
1 egg white
Lemon wedges and chervil sprigs to garnish
Beans and green onions to serve

Season fillets and sprinkle with lemon juice. In a small saucepan, heat wine. Add leek and boil 2 minutes, shaking pan occasionally.

Add lettuce, cover pan, and cook until lettuce has wilted. Uncover pan, increase heat, and heat until excess liquid evaporates. Into a blender or food processor, place lettuce mixture. Add ricotta cheese and process until smooth. Season. Beat egg white until stiff but not dry. Lightly fold in lettuce and cheese mixture.

Place one-quarter of lettuce mixture on one-half of each sole fillet, then fold other half lightly over filling. Place fillets in a steaming basket or large colander. Cover basket or colander, place over a saucepan of boiling water, and steam 10 to 12 minutes or until filling is just set. Let stand 1 to 2 minutes, then, using a pancake turner, carefully transfer to warmed plates. Garnish with lemon wedges and sprigs of chervil and serve with beans and green onions.

Makes 2 to 4 servings.

–FLOUNDER WITH PROSCIUTTO–

2-1/2 large slices prosciutto
8 small flounder fillets
8 small sage leaves
2 tablespoons lemon juice, plus extra for seasoning
Salt and pepper
1-1/2 to 2 tablespoons light olive oil
1 tablespoon unsalted butter, diced
Hot cooked pasta to serve
Lemon peel shreds to garnish

Cut prosciutto into 8 strips lengthwise. On each piece of prosciutto, lay a flounder fillet.

Put a sage leaf at one end of each fillet and season with lemon juice and pepper. Roll up each fillet. Secure each with a wooden pick.

In a nonstick skillet, heat oil. Add flounder rolls, seam sides down, then cook until lightly browned all over. Transfer fish rolls to a warm serving plate. Stir 2 tablespoons lemon juice into pan and bring to a boil. Remove pan from heat and swirl in butter. Season with salt and pepper, then pour over flounder rolls. Serve on a bed of pasta, garnished with lemon peel.

Makes 4 servings.

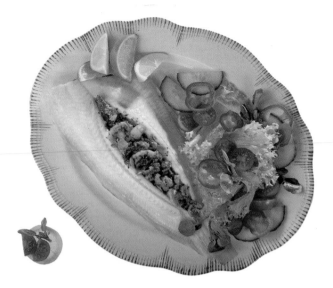

STUFFED SOLE

4 small sole, cleaned and dark skin removed
Salt and pepper
1 tablespoon olive oil
1 small onion, finely chopped
2 garlic cloves, finely crushed
2 cups finely chopped mixed mushrooms, such as
    oyster, shiitake, and button
2 ounces sun-dried tomatoes, thinly sliced
1 cup fresh whole-wheat bread crumbs
1 tablespoon chopped fresh parsley
1 teaspoon chopped fresh marjoram
1 to 2 teaspoons anchovy paste or few drops
    Worcestershire sauce
Mixed salad to serve
Lemon wedges and lime wedges to garnish

Preheat oven to 400F (205C). Butter 1 or 2 baking dishes large enough to hold fish in a single layer. Working with one fish at a time, place fish skinned side uppermost with tail pointing toward you. Run point of filleting knife along line of backbone, then, keeping knife blade firmly against rib bones, slice carefully, lifting fillet as it is freed, until outer edge is almost reached – take care not to pierce through edge, making a pocket.

Repeat with fillet on other side of the backbone. Using sharp small scissors, cut through the top and tail end of backbone and snip bones around edges of fish, taking care not to pierce underskin.

Insert knife point under 1 end of broken backbone, then ease bone away from the under fillets. Lift up bone with attached ribs and remove from fish. Season fish inside and out with salt and pepper. Place in baking dish. Repeat with remaining fish.

In a nonstick skillet, heat oil. Add onion and garlic and cook over medium-low heat until softened but not colored. Add mushrooms and tomatoes and cook over medium heat to evaporate most of the moisture. Stir in bread crumbs, herbs, and anchovy paste or Worcestershire sauce. Season to taste with salt and pepper.

Divide mushroom mixture among pockets in fish. Cover with foil and bake 10 to 20 minutes or until flesh flakes. Serve with mixed salad, garnished with lemon and lime wedges.

Makes 4 servings.

—— FISH & PESTO PACKAGES ——

2 sheets phyllo pastry dough, about 2 ounces
Melted butter for brushing
2 fish fillets, such as turbot or salmon, about 5 ounces
  each, skinned
2 ounces cooked shelled shrimp, finely chopped
1 cup chopped button mushrooms
5 tablespoons fromage frais or low-fat cream cheese
2 to 3 teaspoons pesto sauce
Salt and pepper
Tossed salad to serve

Preheat oven to 400F (205C). Butter a baking sheet. Brush 1 sheet of phyllo pastry with butter. Place the other sheet on top and brush with butter, then cut in half. Place 1 fish fillet in center of each phyllo pastry square. Top with shrimp and mushrooms. Mix together fromage frais or cream cheese and pesto sauce. Season with salt and pepper. Spoon one-quarter of the pesto mixture onto each portion of mushrooms. Reserve remaining mixture.

Bring together 2 opposite edges of phyllo pastry and fold down over fish. Fold remaining edges over and tuck ends under fish. Brush with melted butter and place on baking sheet. Bake 15 minutes or until browned. Using a pancake turner, transfer fish to a warmed serving plate. Split open top of pastry and spoon in remaining pesto mixture. Serve with a tossed salad.

Makes 2 servings.

TURBOT PACKAGES

2 garlic cloves, unpeeled
2 large red bell peppers
2 teaspoons balsamic vinegar
1-1/2 teaspoons olive oil
Salt and pepper
8 spinach leaves, stems removed
4 pieces turbot fillet, about 5-1/2 ounces each
Stir-fried mixed peppers to serve

Preheat broiler. Wrap garlic in foil and broil
5 to 7 minutes to soften. Broil peppers, turning frequently, until evenly charred and
blistered.

Leave peppers until cool enough to handle,
then remove skins. Halve peppers and
remove seeds and cores. Peel garlic. In a
blender or food processor, puree garlic with
peppers, vinegar, and oil. Season with salt
and pepper. To a saucepan of boiling water,
add spinach leaves. Cook 30 seconds. Drain,
and refresh under cold running water, then
spread out on paper towels to dry.

Season turbot. Wrap each piece in 2 spinach
leaves. In a steaming basket or colander,
place wrapped fish and cover. Bring water to
a boil in a saucepan. Place steamer basket on
it and steam 5 to 6 minutes. Meanwhile, heat
pepper sauce gently. Serve sauce with the
turbot packages, accompanied by stir-fried
mixed peppers.

Makes 4 servings.

- FISH WITH MUSHROOM CRUST -

3 cups finely chopped brown mushrooms
2 tablespoons lemon juice
2 tablespoons whole-grain mustard
2 tablespoons firmly packed fresh bread crumbs
3 green onions, finely chopped
1-1/4 tablespoons finely chopped fresh parsley
Salt and pepper
4 turbot fillets, about 5 ounces each
Lemon slices and parsley sprigs to garnish
Zucchini and tomato sautéed together to serve

Preheat broiler. In a bowl, firmly mix together mushrooms, lemon juice, mustard, bread crumbs, green onions, 1 tablespoon of the parsley, and salt and pepper to taste.

Broil turbot, skin sides up, 2 minutes. Turn fish over, spread with mushroom mixture and pat it in.

Broil fish until mushroom mixture has set and fish flakes. Sprinkle with remaining chopped parsley. Garnish with lemon slices and sprigs of parsley and serve with zucchini and tomato sauté.

Makes 4 servings.

-TURBOT WITH ORANGE SAUCE-

4 shallots
1 cup finely chopped fennel
1 small leek, sliced
Small piece gingerroot, sliced
1 turbot fillet, about 12 ounces
2 saffron threads, toasted and crushed
Juice of 2 oranges
1 cup cold unsalted butter, diced
Salt and pepper
Orange slices and fennel or dill sprigs to garnish
Broiled fennel to serve

Finely chop 2 shallots and set aside. Slice remaining shallots.

In a saucepan, place sliced shallots with the fennel, leek, gingerroot, and 2 cups water. Bring to a boil, then cover, remove from heat, and let stand 15 minutes. Transfer 1/2 cup fennel liquid to a small saucepan and set aside. With a slotted spoon, transfer leek and fennel to a steaming basket. Return liquid in saucepan to a boil. Place turbot over leek and fennel. Place over saucepan and cover. Steam 10 minutes.

Meanwhile, into small pan with fennel-flavored liquids, add chopped shallots. Boil until liquid is reduced by two-thirds. Add saffron and orange juice and boil rapidly until reduced by two-thirds. Reduce heat, then gradually beat in butter, beating well after each addition. Season with salt and pepper. Transfer fish to a warm serving plate, discarding leek and fennel. Pour sauce over fish and garnish with orange slices and fennel or dill sprigs. Serve with broiled fennel.

Makes 2 servings.

──HALIBUT WITH ZUCCHINI──

2-2/3 cups thinly sliced small zucchini
4 halibut fillets, 5 to 6 ounces each
4 tablespoons unsalted butter (optional)
Finely grated peel and juice of 1 lemon
Salt and pepper
4 sprigs chervil
Lemon wedges and chervil sprigs to garnish

Preheat oven to 350F (175C). Generously butter 4 pieces of parchment paper or foil large enough to loosely enclose each fillet.

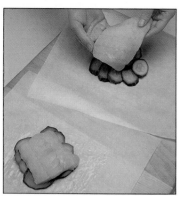

Bring a saucepan of salted water to a boil. Add zucchini and boil 1 minute. Drain and refresh under cold running water. Pat dry. Make a bed of zucchini in center of each piece of paper or foil. Place a piece of fish on each bed of zucchini. Place about 1 tablespoon of butter, if using, on each fillet. Sprinkle with lemon peel and juice, season with salt and pepper, and top with a chervil sprig.

Fold paper or foil over fish and seal edges tightly. Place fish packages on a baking sheet and bake about 15 minutes. Either serve fish and zucchini in the packages or transfer, with cooking juices, to warm plates. Garnish with lemon wedges and sprigs of chervil.

Makes 4 servings.

——— HALIBUT WITH PAPRIKA ———

4 teaspoons olive oil
6 ounces shiitake mushrooms, sliced
Salt and pepper
1-1/4 pounds halibut fillets, cut into 1/2-inch strips
1 onion, thinly sliced
1 large red bell pepper, seeded and thinly sliced
2 garlic cloves, finely chopped
2 teaspoons paprika
1 teaspoon all-purpose flour
Pinch dried leaf oregano, crumbled
1/2 cup fish stock
1/2 cup plain yogurt
Hot cooked rice to serve
Chopped fresh parsley to garnish

In a nonstick skillet, heat 2 teaspoons of the oil. Add mushrooms and cook over low heat 5 minutes. Season with salt and pepper and cook 1 minute longer. Transfer to a plate. Add fish to pan and sauté 2 to 3 minutes or until just cooked through. Transfer to a plate. Add remaining oil to pan. Heat, then add onion, bell pepper, and garlic. Stir-fry until softened. Stir in paprika and cook 1 minute longer.

Into pan, sprinkle flour. Stir in oregano and stock. Cover and cook 10 minutes, stirring occasionally. To a blender or food processor, transfer half of the pepper and onion mixture. Add yogurt and puree. Return to pan with mushrooms and any accumulated juices. Reheat gently, without boiling. Add fish and warm through. Serve on a bed of rice, garnished with parsley.

Makes 4 servings.

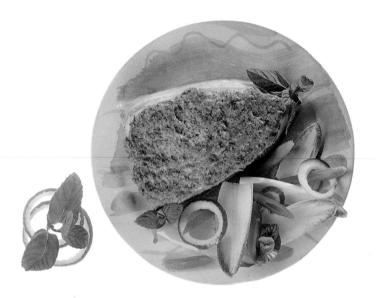

—YOGURT-TOPPED HALIBUT—

2 tablespoons cumin seeds
2 tablespoons coriander seeds
2 large green onions, chopped
2 garlic cloves, chopped
2 tablespoons chopped fresh mint
2 teaspoons dried dill weed
2/3 cup plain yogurt
1 teaspoon paprika
Salt and pepper
4 halibut steaks, about 6 ounces each
Mint sprigs to garnish
Belgian endive, red onion, and mint salad to serve

Heat a small, heavy skillet. Add cumin and coriander seeds and heat until fragrant.

Into a mortar or small bowl, place seeds. Crush with a pestle or end of a rolling pan. Work in green onions, garlic, mint, and dill, then stir in yogurt and paprika. Season with salt and pepper.

Into a shallow baking, place fish in a single layer. Spread yogurt mixture over top of each steak, cover dish, and refrigerate 2 to 3 hours. Preheat broiler. Broil fish, basting occasionally, 10 to 15 minutes or until fish begins to flake and a crust has formed on yogurt topping. Garnish with sprigs of mint and serve salad.

Makes 4 servings.

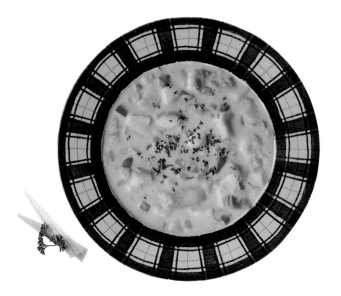

CHOWDER

1/4 cup butter
1 large onion, chopped
2 large garlic cloves, chopped
6 stalks celery, chopped
1 pound potatoes, cut into small chunks
Large pinch red (cayenne) pepper
2-1/2 cups fish stock
2-1/2 cups milk
Bouquet garni
8 ounces smoked haddock fillet
8 ounces fresh haddock fillet
4 ounces shelled cooked shrimp
1/2 red bell pepper, seeded and diced
1 cup whole-kernel corn (optional)
Salt and black pepper
Chopped fresh parsley or dill to garnish

In a large saucepan, melt butter. Add onion, garlic, and celery and cook until beginning to soften. Stir in potatoes and cayenne and cook about 2 minutes, stirring occasionally. Add stock, milk, and bouquet garni. Bring to a boil, then cover pan and simmer about 20 minutes or until vegetables are almost tender.

Meanwhile, skin both types of haddock and cut into bite-size pieces. Add to saucepan and simmer gently 5 to 10 minutes or until fish begins flakes. Stir in shrimp, bell pepper, and corn, if using. Heat through. Season with salt and black pepper. Serve sprinkled with parsley.

Makes 4 to 6 servings.

— HADDOCK & PARSLEY SAUCE —

4 haddock fillets, about 6 ounces each
1/4 cup butter
3 tablespoons lemon juice
2/3 cup fish stock
1 bay leaf
Salt and pepper
4 teaspoons all-purpose flour
2/3 cup milk
1/4 cup whipping cream
1 egg yolk
4 tablespoons chopped fresh parsley
Green beans, lemon wedges, and parsley sprigs to serve

Into a skillet, place fish. Add half the butter, the lemon juice, stock, and bay leaf.

Season with salt and pepper. Slowly bring to a simmer, then reduce heat, cover pan, and poach fish 10 to 15 minutes, depending on thickness, until flesh just begins to flake. Meanwhile, in a saucepan, melt remaining butter. Stir in flour, then cook, stirring, 1 minute. Gradually stir in milk, then bring to a boil, stirring. Simmer about 4 minutes, stirring frequently. Blend cream into egg yolk. Remove pan from heat and stir in egg mixture and parsley. Reheat gently, stirring constantly, a few minutes; do not boil.

Transfer fish to a warmed serving plate, cover, and keep warm. Remove sauce from heat and strain in fish cooking liquid, mixing together well. Discard bay leaf, then pour into a warmed sauce boat to serve with the fish. Serve with green beans and lemon wedges, garnished with sprigs of parsley.

Makes 4 servings.

— HADDOCK WITH TOMATOES —

4 tomatoes
4 tablespoons virgin olive oil, plus extra for skillet
1 shallot, finely chopped
1 small garlic clove, finely chopped
Juice of 1 small lemon
1 teaspoon Dijon mustard
2 tablespoons snipped fresh chives
2 teaspoons chopped fresh parsley
Salt and pepper
4 haddock fillets
Snipped fresh chives and salad greens to garnish

Preheat broiler. Place tomatoes about 6 inches from heat source and broil until the entire skin is blistered and lightly charred, turning them frequently. Remove charred patches and any skin that comes off easily. Halve tomatoes and remove seeds, then dice flesh. In a saucepan, heat 1 tablespoon oil. Add shallot and garlic and stir-fry until softened. Stir in lemon juice and mustard, then beat in remaining oil. Add tomatoes and herbs and season with salt and pepper. Keep sauce warm over low heat; do not boil.

Heat a nonstick skillet and brush generously with oil. Add fish, skin sides down, and cook about 3 minutes or until skins begin to crisp. Turn fish over and cook 2 minutes longer. Spoon sauce onto warmed plates. Place fish on sauce. Garnish with snipped chives and salad greens.

Makes 4 servings.

—COD WITH TERIYAKI GLAZE—

2 tablespoons soy sauce
1 tablespoon rice wine or medium-dry sherry
1 tablespoon light brown sugar
1 teaspoon grated gingerroot
4 cod fillets with skin
Chervil sprigs to garnish
Stir-fried vegetables to serve

In a small saucepan, combine soy sauce, rice wine or sherry, sugar, and gingerroot. Simmer 2 to 3 minutes or until lightly syrupy. Let cool.

Preheat broiler. Broil fish, skin sides down, 3 minutes. Turn fish over and broil 3 to 4 minutes, until skin is crisp and flesh almost cooked through.

Turn fish over, and brush top liberally with sauce. Return to broiler 1 minute. Transfer fish to warm serving plates and pour any remaining sauce over fish. Garnish with sprigs of chervil and serve with stir-fried vegetables.

Makes 4 servings.

— BAKED COD WITH LENTILS —

3 tablespoons olive oil
3 shallots, finely chopped
2 garlic cloves, finely crushed
1 cup green or brown lentils
3-1/2 teaspoons crushed coriander seeds
1-1/4 cups fish stock
1-1/4 cups dry white wine
2 tablespoons chopped fresh cilantro
1-1/2 pounds cod fillet, cut into 4 pieces
Pinch saffron threads, toasted and crushed
4 tomatoes, peeled, seeded, and chopped
Salt and pepper
Cilantro sprigs to garnish

In a saucepan, heat 1-1/2 tablespoons oil. Add 2 of the shallots and the garlic and cook over low heat until softened. Stir in lentils and 3 teaspoons coriander seeds. Cook 2 minutes, stirring, then stir in stock and wine. Bring to a boil, then reduce heat and simmer, covered, 30 to 45 minutes until lentils are tender. Stir in chopped cilantro. Meanwhile, preheat oven to 450F (230C). In a nonstick roasting pan, heat 1 tablespoon oil. Add cod, skin sides down; cook 2 minutes. Transfer to oven and bake 8 minutes.

In a saucepan, heat remaining oil. Add remaining shallot and coriander seeds and the saffron and cook over low heat until softened. Add tomatoes and a little lentil cooking liquid, then season with salt and pepper. Simmer 5 minutes. Drain lentils and season. Serve cod on lentils, garnished with sprigs of cilantro and accompanied by the tomato relish.

Makes 4 servings.

FISH CAKES

1 pound potatoes, cut into pieces and boiled
1 pound cooked mixed fresh and smoked fish, such as
    haddock or cod, flaked
2 tablespoons butter, diced
3 tablespoons chopped fresh parsley
1 egg, separated
Salt and pepper
1 egg, beaten
About 1 cup bread crumbs made from day-old bread
Olive oil for frying
Lemon wedges and onion and avocado salad to serve
Dill sprigs to garnish

Drain potatoes. Gently heat potatoes in saucepan a few minutes over low heat, shaking pan occasionally.

Remove pan from heat. Mash potatoes, then beat in fish, butter, chopped parsley, and egg yolk. Season with salt and pepper. Transfer to a large bowl and mix well. Chill if the mixture is too soft to handle.

Divide fish mixture into 8 equal portions. With floured hands, form each portion into a flat cake. In a bowl, beat egg white with whole egg. Spread bread crumbs on a plate. Dip each fish cake in egg, then in bread crumbs. In a skillet, heat a thin layer of oil. Fry fish cakes about 3 minutes on each side until crisp and golden. Drain on paper towels. Serve hot with lemon wedges and salad, garnished with sprigs of dill.

Makes 4 servings.

FISH GRATINS

1/2 teaspoon Dijon mustard
1 tablespoon lemon juice
1 tablespoon olive oil
Pinch freshly grated nutmeg
Salt and pepper
4 cod or haddock steaks, about 5 ounces each
1/2 cup finely shredded sharp Cheddar cheese
3 tablespoons freshly grated Parmesan cheese
2 tablespoons fine fresh bread crumbs
Paprika
Pattypan squash to serve
Basil sprigs to garnish

Preheat broiler. In a small bowl, beat together mustard and lemon juice using a fork, then gradually beat in oil. Add nutmeg and season with salt and pepper. Place fish in a broiler pan. Brush 1 side of each fish with mustard mixture, then broil, coated sides up, 2 minutes. Turn fish over, brush tops with mustard mixture, and broil 2 minutes longer.

Cover fish with Cheddar cheese. Mix together Parmesan cheese and bread crumbs, then sprinkle evenly over fish. Season generously with pepper. Broil until the top is golden and bubbling. Lightly sprinkle with paprika. Serve with pattypan squash, garnished with sprigs of basil.

Makes 4 servings.

FISH FINGERS WITH PIQUANT DIP

1-1/4 pounds firm white fish, such as hake, haddock, or
  cod, skinned
Salt and pepper
1 egg, beaten
1 cup fresh bread crumbs
Olive oil for deep-frying
Lemon wedges and dill sprigs to garnish
DIP:
2/3 cup low-fat mayonnaise
6 tablespoons plain yogurt
3-1/2 tablespoons finely chopped dill pickles
2 tablespoons chopped dill
1 tablespoon capers, drained and chopped if large
2 teaspoons Dijon mustard

To make dip, in a bowl, beat all ingredients
together. Pour into a serving bowl, cover,
and refrigerate.

Remove bones from fish, then cut flesh into
thin strips. Season strips. Dip in egg, then in
bread crumbs to coat evenly. Half-fill a deep-
fat fryer with oil and heat to 350F (175C).
Add fish, in batches if necessary so pan is not
crowded, and fry until crisp and golden.
Drain on paper towels. Serve hot with
wooden picks, accompanied by the dip.
Garnish with lemon wedges ad sprigs of dill.

Makes 4 servings.

HOT FISH LOAF

3 tablespoons butter
2 garlic cloves, crushed
2 teaspoons all-purpose flour
3/4 cup milk
1-1/4 pounds white fish fillets, such as cod or haddock,
   skinned and chopped
2/3 cup whipping cream
2 teaspoons anchovy extract
3 eggs and 1 egg yolk
Lemon juice
Salt and red (cayenne) pepper
4 ounces cooked shelled shrimp
2 tablespoons chopped fresh basil
Lemon wedges and cilantro sprigs to garnish
Cheese, tomato, or broccoli sauce to serve (optional)

Preheat oven to 300F (150C). Butter and line bottom of a 6-1/2-cup terrine or loaf pan. In a saucepan, melt butter. Add garlic and cook 1 minute. Stir in flour and cook, stirring, 1 minute, then gradually stir in milk. Bring to a boil, stirring. Reduce heat and simmer about 3 minutes, stirring occasionally. Pour sauce into a blender or food processor. Add fish, cream, anchovy extract, eggs, and egg yolk. Puree, then add lemon juice and salt and cayenne.

Spoon half the fish mixture into terrine or loaf pan. Finely chop shrimp, then sprinkle them evenly over fish with chopped basil. Spoon remaining fish mixture over top. Cover terrine or loaf pan tightly with parchment paper or foil. Place in a roasting pan and pour in enough boiling water to come halfway up sides. Bake about 1-3/4 hours. Onto a warm serving plate, invert terrine or pan. Tilt slightly to drain off juice. Garnish with lemon and cilantro and serve with sauce, if desired.

Makes 4 to 6 servings.

WHITING WITH ITALIAN SAUCE

3 tablespoons olive oil
4 whiting fillets, 6 to 7 ounces each
2 onions, finely chopped
1 or 2 anchovy fillets, coarsely chopped
3 tablespoons chopped fresh parsley
3/4 cup dry white wine
Pepper
Parsley sprigs to garnish
Orange, cherry tomato, and green onion salad to serve

In a skillet, heat oil. Add fish and fry 2 to 3 minutes on each side until almost cooked.

Transfer fish to paper towels, cover, and keep warm. Add onions to skillet and cook over medium heat until lightly colored. Stir in anchovies and parsley, stirring until anchovies dissolve, then add wine. Boil until reduced by half.

Carefully return fish to skillet. Baste with sauce, season with pepper, and heat 2 to 3 minutes, basting occasionally. Serve garnished with sprigs of parsley, accompanied by salad.

Makes 4 servings.

— SESAME-COATED WHITING —

1 tablespoon Dijon mustard
1 tablespoon tomato paste
1-1/2 teaspoons finely chopped fresh tarragon
Squeeze of lemon juice
Pepper
1/2 cup sesame seeds
2 tablespoons all-purpose flour
1 egg, lightly beaten
4 whiting fillets, about 5 ounces each, skinned
Olive oil for brushing
Red bell pepper, zucchini, and leeks to serve
Tarragon sprigs and lemon wedges to garnish

In a small bowl, mix mustard, tomato paste, tarragon, lemon juice, and pepper.

Combine sesame seeds and flour and spread evenly on a large plate. Pour egg into a shallow bowl. Spread mustard mixture over both sides of each fish fillet, then dip fillet in egg. Coat fish evenly in sesame seed and flour mixture, then refrigerate 30 minutes.

Preheat broiler. Oil a broiler pan. Place coated fillets on broiler pan. Brush 1 side of each fillet lightly with oil, then broil 2 minutes. Turn fish over, lightly brush top with oil and broil 2 minutes longer. Using a pancake turner, transfer fish to a warm serving plate. Serve with red bell pepper, zucchini, and leeks, garnished with sprigs of tarragon and lemon wedges.

Makes 4 servings.

— WHITING WITH SPINACH —

2 tablespoons butter
1 tablespoon light olive oil
1 small onion, finely chopped
3 cups sliced button mushrooms
2 pounds spinach, stems removed
Pinch freshly grated nutmeg
Salt and pepper
4 whiting fillets, skinned and halved lengthwise
2 tablespoons freshly grated Parmesan cheese
Dill sprigs and shavings of Parmesan cheese to garnish

Preheat oven to 350F (175C). Butter a shallow baking dish. In a nonstick skillet, heat oil. Add onion and cook over low heat until softened but not browned.

Increase heat. Add mushrooms and cook 2 to 3 minutes. Add spinach to pan and heat, stirring frequently, until no excess liquid is visible. Add butter and season with nutmeg, salt, and pepper.

Spread spinach mixture in baking dish. Season whiting, roll up with skinned sides in, and secure with wooden picks. Arrange whiting on top of spinach mixture. Sprinkle with grated Parmesan cheese, cover, and bake 20 to 25 minutes. Serve garnished with sprigs of dill and Parmesan cheese.

Makes 4 servings.

MONKFISH IN COCONUT CREAM

Seeds from 4 or 5 cardamom pods
3/4 teaspoon coriander seeds
1/2-3/4 teaspoon cumin seeds
Generous 1/2-inch piece gingerroot, finely chopped
1 large or 2 small stalks lemon grass, crushed and finely
    chopped
Salt and pepper
2 pounds monkfish
2 shallots
1 garlic clove
1 ounce creamed coconut, chopped
2/3 cup hot water
Chinese noodles, baby corn, and baby zucchini to serve
Lemon slices to garnish

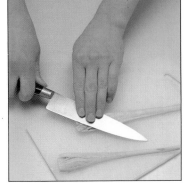

Preheat oven to 350F (175C). Heat a heavy pan. Add cardamom, coriander, and cumin seeds and heat until fragrant. Into a mortar or small bowl, place seeds. Crush finely with pestle or end of a rolling pin. Crush in ginger, lemon grass, and pepper. Remove fine skin and the bone from monkfish. Cut flesh into 4 pieces and rub spice mixture into them. Marinate 30 minutes.

Finely chop shallots and garlic together. Sprinkle half into a shallow baking dish just large enough to hold fish. Place fish on shallot mixture and scatter remaining mixture over the top. Blend coconut with water until smooth. Pour over fish. Season with salt and pepper, then cover and bake about 30 minutes or until fish flakes. Serve with Chinese noodles, baby corn, and zucchini, garnished with lemon slices.

Makes 4 servings.

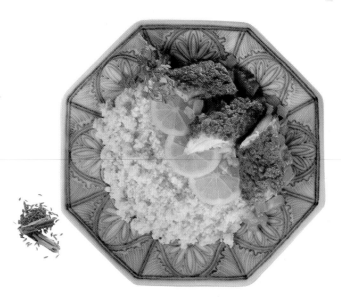

—MIDDLE EASTERN MONKFISH—

2 garlic cloves
1 (2-1/2-inch) piece gingerroot
3 tablespoons olive oil
2-1/2 tablespoons tomato paste
1-1/2 teaspoons ground cinnamon
1 teaspoon caraway seeds, crushed
Salt and pepper
2-1/4 pounds monkfish
1/2 onion, finely chopped
Couscous and lemon slices to serve

Finely chop garlic and gingerroot together. In a small bowl, stir oil into tomato paste. Stir in garlic mixture, cinnamon, and caraway seeds. Season with salt and pepper.

Remove fine skin from monkfish, then spread with spice mixture. Place fish into a shallow dish. Cover and refrigerate 1 to 1-1/2 hours.

Preheat oven to 400F (205C). Cut a piece of foil large enough to enclose fish. Make a bed of chopped onion on foil. Place monkfish, and any spice paste left in dish, on onion. Fold foil loosely over fish and seal edges tightly. Bake monkfish 20 to 25 minutes. Open foil, baste fish, and bake 10 to 15 minutes longer or until fish flakes. Serve on a bed of couscous, garnished with lemon slices.

Makes 4 servings.

— CHUNKY FISH CASSEROLE —

1 cup pasta shells
3 tablespoons olive oil
2 garlic cloves, finely crushed
1/2 cup pearl onions, halved
2 cups halved button mushrooms
1 pound firm, white fish, such as cod or monkfish
8 ounces trout fillets
3 tablespoons well-seasoned all-purpose flour
1-1/3 cups fava beans
1/2 cup dry white wine
1-1/4 cups fish stock
Large bouquet garni
Grated peel and juice of 1 lemon
5 ounces cooked shelled shrimp or cooked shelled
    mussels or clams
Chopped fresh herbs to garnish

Preheat oven to 350F (175C). In a large saucepan of boiling water, cook pasta three-quarters of time recommended on package. Drain and rinse under cold running water; set aside. In a skillet, heat half the oil. Add garlic, onions, and mushrooms and cook 3 to 4 minutes. Using a slotted spoon, transfer vegetables to a large, deep baking dish. Meanwhile, skin fish, if needed, and cut into 1-inch chunks. Toss in seasoned flour.

Heat remaining oil in a skillet. Add fish, in batches if necessary, and fry 2 to 3 minutes, turning pieces carefully. Transfer to dish. Add pasta and beans. Stir wine, stock, bouquet garni, and lemon peel and juice into skillet. Bring to a boil. Reduce heat and simmer a few minutes, then pour into dish. Cover and bake about 30 minutes. Add shrimp, mussels or clams, cover again, and bake about 5 minutes. Garnish with plenty of chopped herbs.

Makes 4 servings.

—MONKFISH ON RATATOUILLE—

2 eggplants, halved lengthwise
3 zucchini, sliced
Salt and pepper
2 monkfish tails, total weight about 2-1/2 pounds
6 garlic cloves
5 tablespoons olive oil
1 Spanish onion, very thinly sliced
2 large red bell peppers, thinly sliced
4 large tomatoes, peeled, seeded, and chopped
Leaves from a few sprigs of thyme, marjoram, and
    oregano
About 2 tablespoons each chopped parsley and torn
    basil

Cut eggplants into 1-inch slices. Into a colander, put eggplant slices and zucchini slices. Sprinkle with salt and let stand 1 hour. Rinse well, then pat dry with paper towels.

Meanwhile, remove fine skin from monkfish and cut slits in flesh. Cut 3 garlic cloves into thin slivers, then insert in slits. Season with salt and pepper and set aside. Chop remaining garlic.

In a heavy large saucepan, heat 2 tablespoons oil. Add eggplant slices and sauté a few minutes. Add another tablespoon oil and the onion and chopped garlic and sauté a few minutes. Add bell peppers and cook 1 minute, stirring occasionally.

Add 2 more tablespoons oil and zucchini. Cook, stirring occasionally, a few minutes, then add tomatoes. Snip in herb leaves and season with salt and pepper. Cover and simmer 30 to 40 minutes, stirring occasionally, or until fairly dry.

Meanwhile, preheat oven to 400F (205C). Stir parsley into ratatouille. Turn ratatouille into a baking dish. Lay monkfish on top and bake, uncovered, 30 to 40 minutes, turning fish occasionally, or until fish flakes. Sprinkle with basil just before end of cooking.

Makes 4 to 6 servings.

CEVICHE

1 pound monkfish or halibut fillets, thinly sliced
1 fresh red chile, seeded and thinly sliced
2 teaspoons coriander seeds, toasted and finely crushed
Salt
Juice of 4 limes
2-1/2 tablespoons virgin olive oil
1/2 red onion, thinly sliced
1 beefsteak tomato, peeled, seeded, and cut into thin
    strips
1 red bell pepper, seeded and chopped
1 tablespoon chopped cilantro
Lime wedges to garnish
Mâche and red Belgian endive salad to serve

In a shallow, nonmetallic dish, lay fish in a single layer. Scatter chile and coriander seeds over fish and sprinkle with salt. Pour lime juice over fish. Cover and refrigerate 2 to 4 hours.

Drain off juices from fish and mix 2-1/2 tablespoons juice with the oil; discard remaining juices. Scatter onion, tomato, bell pepper, and chopped cilantro over fish. Drizzle oil mixture over the vegetables and fish. Serve garnished with lime wedges and accompanied by salad.

Makes 4 appetizer servings.

BROILED FISH & CILANTRO

1-1/2 pounds gray mullet, porgy, or monkfish fillets
3 tablespoons olive oil
2 garlic cloves, crushed
1-1/2 teaspoons toasted cumin seeds, ground
1 teaspoon paprika
1 fresh green chile, finely chopped
Handful cilantro leaves, finely chopped
3 tablespoons lime juice
Salt
Hot cooked rice to serve
Mint sprigs and lime wedges to serve

Place fish into a shallow, nonmetallic dish. In a bowl, mix together remaining ingredients, except rice, mint and lime wedges.

Spoon olive oil mixture over fish. Cover and refrigerate 3 to 4 hours, turning occasionally.

Preheat broiler. Place fish on a baking sheet. Broil fish about 4 minutes on each side, basting with cilantro mixture occasionally, until flesh flakes when tested with the point of a sharp knife. Serve warm on a bed of rice, garnished with sprigs of mint and lime wedges.

Makes 4 servings.

– HAKE BAKED WITH POTATOES –

1 pound yellow potatoes, very thinly sliced, rinsed, and
  dried
1 red bell pepper, cored and seeded
1 onion, thinly sliced
1 large tomato, chopped
3 garlic cloves, slivered
1/2 cup chopped fresh parsley
Salt and pepper
1 cup fish stock or water
1-1/2 pounds hake cutlets with skin, 1 inch thick
1 bay leaf
3 sprigs thyme
4 thin lemon slices
1 tablespoon olive oil
1/4 cup dry sherry
Oregano sprigs to garnish

Preheat oven to 375F (190C). In a large,
lightly oiled baking dish, place half the
potatoes. Chop bell pepper, then scatter it
over potatoes with onion, tomato, garlic, and
parsley. Season with salt and pepper. Cover
with remaining potato slices. Pour stock over
vegetable mixture, cover dish, and bake 1
hour. Increase oven temperature to 425F
(220C), uncover dish, and bake about 7
minutes longer.

Season fish. Place bay leaf and thyme on
potatoes, then place fish on top and nestle it
into potatoes. Lay lemon slices on fish, drizzle
oil over the top and return to oven 8 minutes
until potatoes are crisp and brown. Spoon
sherry over fish and return to oven 2 minutes.
Discard bay leaf and thyme. Serve garnished
with sprigs of oregano.

Makes 4 servings.

– RED SNAPPER WITH CROSTINI –

4 red snapper fillets
4-1/2 tablespoons olive oil
5 black peppercorns, coarsely crushed
1 orange, peeled and thinly sliced
Juice of 1 lemon
1 small fennel bulb, quartered
Salt and pepper
8 thin slices French bread
2 garlic cloves, cut in half
3 or 4 anchovy fillets
Juice of 1/2 orange
Fennel sprigs and orange slices to garnish

With a skewer, prick fish. In a shallow, non-metallic dish, lay fish in a single layer.

Pour 2-1/2 tablespoons olive oil over fish. Add peppercorns and orange slices. Cover and refrigerate, turning occasionally. In a small saucepan of boiling water, with lemon juice added, cook fennel until soft. Drain fennel, then, in a food processor or blender, puree with 1/2 tablespoon olive oil. Season with salt and pepper and keep warm. Rub bread with cut surfaces of garlic, then fry in remaining olive oil. Keep warm.

Drain fish and reserve marinade. In a skillet, heat 1-1/2 tablespoons marinade. Add fish and cook about 3 minutes each side. Transfer to a warm plate and keep warm. Add anchovies to pan, crushing them into oil, then add orange juice and heat through. Season with pepper, then pour over fish. Spread fennel puree on bread and serve with fish. Garnish with sprigs of fennel and orange slices.

Makes 2 to 4 servings.

— BREAM WITH TARRAGON —

2 tablespoons white-wine vinegar
1-1/2 to 2 teaspoons Dijon mustard
1 small shallot, finely chopped
1 garlic clove, finely crushed
1/2 cup olive oil, plus extra for brushing
14 ounces tomatoes, peeled, seeded, and diced
1-1/2 tablespoons chopped fresh tarragon
2 tablespoons finely snipped fresh chives
Salt and pepper
Pinch sugar (optional)
4 red bream or porgy, about 10 ounces each
4 sprigs tarragon
Tarragon sprigs and lime wedges to garnish

In a blender, blend together vinegar, mustard, shallot, and garlic until mixture thickens. Gradually add oil through lid while motor runs. Transfer to a bowl. Add tomatoes, tarragon, and chives. Season with salt and pepper. Add a pinch of sugar, if using, then let stand 30 to 60 minutes.

Preheat broiler. With the point of a sharp knife, cut 2 slashes on each side of fish. Season fish, put a tarragon sprig in each cavity, and brush with oil. Place fish in a baking pan. Broil 10 to 11 minutes, turning and brushing with oil once, or until fish flakes. Transfer to serving plates. Stir tomato mixture, spoon some onto fish and serve remaining separately. Garnish with sprigs of tarragon and lime wedges.

Makes 4 servings.

—SEA BASS UNDER A CRUST—

1 (2-lb.) sea bass, cleaned but not scaled, fins trimmed
4 or 5 herb sprigs, such as tarragon, basil, fennel, and
    parsley
5 black peppercorns, crushed
4 pounds coarse sea salt
Tomato, basil, red onion, and caper salad to serve
Lemon wedges and basil sprigs to garnish

Preheat oven to 425F (220C). In cavity of sea bass, place herb sprigs and peppercorns. In a deep baking dish that fish will fit without too much space around, spread a layer of salt about 1 inch deep.

Place fish on salt. Pack salt around fish until it is completely buried and there is a 1-inch layer on top. Bake fish about 25 minutes.

To serve, crack open salt crust and remove pieces carefully to expose whole fish. Remove skin from top of fish and serve the fish with salad, garnished with lemon wedges and sprigs of basil.

Makes 2 or 3 servings.

SEA BASS & GARLIC

1-1/2 tablespoons unsalted butter
8 garlic cloves, lightly crushed
16 green onions, sliced
4 sea bass fillets with skin, about 7 ounces each
Salt and pepper
2 slices lean smoked slab bacon, cut into thin strips
1 sprig thyme
1/2 cup fish stock
1 tablespoon chopped fresh parsley
Tarragon sprigs to garnish
Boiled new potatoes to serve

Preheat oven to 400F (205C). In a heavy, shallow flameproof pan, melt butter. Add garlic and green onions and cook over low heat until browned. Season skin side of fish, then add to casserole, skin side down, with bacon and thyme. Cook about 2 minutes, then turn fish over and add stock.

Bake 4 to 6 minutes or until fish flakes. Discard thyme. Stir in parsley, and add seasoning if necessary. Garnish with sprigs of tarragon and serve with new potatoes.

Makes 4 servings.

— BASS WITH GINGER & LIME —

2 shallots, finely chopped
1 (1-1/2-inch) piece gingerroot, finely chopped
Juice of 2 limes
1/4 cup rice wine vinegar
1 cup olive oil
2 tablespoons Chinese sesame oil
2 tablespoons soy sauce
Salt and pepper
6 to 8 bass fillets, about 1/2 inch thick each
Leaves from 1 bunch cilantro
Toasted sesame seeds to garnish
Stir-fried baby corn and sun-dried tomatoes to serve

In a bowl, mix together first 8 ingredients.
Set aside.

Preheat broiler. Brush fish lightly with ginger
mixture. Place fish on a large baking sheet.
Broil 2 to 3 minutes on each side.

Before serving, bring remaining ginger
mixture to a full boil, then remove from heat.
Chop cilantro, reserving a few leaves for
garnish. Mix chopped cilantro into ginger
mixture. Spoon some onto serving plates at
room temperature, then place fish on top.
Sprinkle with sesame seeds and garnish with
reserved cilantro leaves. Serve with stir-fried
baby corn and sun-dried tomatoes.

Makes 6 to 8 servings.

SPICED BASS

4 sea bass steaks, 5 to 6 ounces each
Zucchini and green onion salad to serve
Lemon peel and cilantro sprigs to garnish
MARINADE:
1 (1/2-inch) piece gingerroot
1 garlic clove
2 green onions, sliced
1 tablespoon lime juice
1 tablespoon sesame oil
2 tablespoons grapeseed oil
1/2 teaspoon Chinese five-spice powder
2 tablespoons sake or dry sherry

To make marinade, in a blender or small food processor, process gingerroot, garlic, green onions, and lime juice together to make a paste. With motor running, slowly pour in oils, then add five-spice powder and sake or sherry.

Arrange fish steaks in a single layer in a nonmetallic dish. Pour marinade over fish, then marinate 1 hour in the refrigerator. Preheat broiler. Remove fish from marinade and place in a baking pan. Broil about 4 minutes on each side, brushing with marinade when fish is turned. Serve with salad, garnished with lemon peel and cilantro sprigs.

Makes 4 servings.

–TROUT WITH TOMATO SAUCE–

2-1/2 ounces sun-dried tomatoes
2 teaspoons capers, drained
1 large garlic clove, crushed
8 basil leaves
Leaves from 2 small sprigs rosemary
Leaves from 2 sprigs oregano
1/4 cup butter, plus extra for brushing
1 tablespoon crème fraîche or sour cream
1-1/4 cup fish stock
Salt and pepper
6 to 8 trout fillets
Sugar snap peas and sun-dried tomatoes to serve
Lemon wedges and oregano sprigs to garnish

In a blender or food processor, process sun-dried tomatoes, capers, garlic, herbs, 1/4 cup butter, crème fraîche, and stock until smooth. Season with pepper and just a little salt. Pour mixture into a saucepan.

Preheat broiler. Brush trout with butter and season with pepper. Place on a baking sheet and broil 3 to 4 minutes on each side. Meanwhile, heat sauce over low heat, stirring occasionally. Transfer fish to warm plates, season with salt and spoon sauce over the fish. Serve with sugar snap peas and sun-dried tomatoes, garnished with lemon wedges and sprigs of oregano.

Makes 3 or 4 servings.

— TROUT WITH HAZELNUTS —

2/3 cup hazelnuts in their shells
5 tablespoons butter
4 trout, about 10 ounces each
Salt and pepper
2 tablespoons lemon juice
Lemon wedges and parsley sprigs to garnish
Orange and lollo lettuce salad to serve

Preheat broiler. Shell hazelnuts, then spread in a single layer in a broiler pan. Broil, stirring frequently, until skins split. Turn nuts onto a dish and rub to remove skins. Chop nuts.

In a large skillet, melt 4 tablespoons of the butter. Season trout inside and out with salt and pepper, then add 2 trout to pan. Fry 12 to 15 minutes, turning once, until brown and fish begins to flake. Drain fish on paper towels, then transfer to a warm serving plate and keep warm while frying remaining fish in the same way.

Wipe pan with paper towel. Melt remaining butter in skillet. Add chopped nuts and cook until browned. Stir lemon juice into pan. Quickly pour mixture over fish. Garnish with lemon wedges and sprigs of parsley. Serve with salad.

Makes 4 servings.

— TROUT WITH PROSCIUTTO —

4 trout, about 10 ounces each
Pepper
1 lemon, quartered
4 sprigs basil or tarragon
4 slices prosciutto
Lemon wedges and chervil sprigs to garnish
Tomato, lime, red chicory, and asparagus salad to serve

Preheat oven to 400F (205C). Season trout with pepper and a squeeze of lemon juice. Inside each fish, place a sprig of basil or tarragon.

Wrap a slice of prosciutto around each fish and season with pepper. Place fish into a large shallow baking dish with loose ends of prosciutto underneath.

Bake fish 15 to 20 minutes or until cooked through and flesh flakes. Garnish with lemon wedges and sprigs of chervil and serve with salad.

Makes 4 servings.

CURRIED TROUT

Seeds from 6 cardamom pods
2 teaspoons cumin seeds
1/4 cup plain yogurt
1 large garlic clove, chopped
2 tablespoons lime juice
1 (1-inch) piece gingerroot, chopped
1 teaspoon curry powder
Pinch ground turmeric
1/4 teaspoon red (cayenne) pepper
Salt
1 teaspoon red food coloring (optional)
2 trout, about 10 ounces each
Vegetable oil for brushing
Rice with chiles and tomato and onion salad
Lemon and lime wedges and cilantro sprigs to garnish

Heat a small, heavy pan. Add cardamom and cumin seeds and heat until fragrant. Into a mortar or small bowl, place seeds. Crush with a pestle or end of a rolling pin. Into a blender or small food processor, put yogurt, garlic, lime juice, all the spices, cayenne, and salt. Mix together to make a paste. Add food coloring, if using.

With the point of a sharp knife, make 3 deep slashes in each side of trout. Spread spice mixture over trout, working it into the slashes. Place trout into a shallow, non-metallic dish in a single layer. Cover and marinate in refrigerator 4 hours. Preheat broiler. Brush broiler tray with oil. Sprinkle a little oil over fish and broil about 7 minutes on each side. Serve with rice, chiles, tomato and onion salad, garnished with lemon and lime wedges and sprigs of cilantro.

Makes 2 servings.

TROUT & ARTICHOKE FRITTATA

1 medium or 2 small artichokes
3 tablespoons unsalted butter
6 eggs
7 ounces cooked, skinned trout fillet, flaked
2 tablespoons chopped fresh parsley
Salt and pepper
Green salad to serve
Lemon wedges and parsley sprigs to garnish

Snap off artichoke stems, then bend outer leaves backward to remove them. Continue until pale inner cone is reached. Cut off tough top part of cone and remove hairy inner choke. Trim artichoke, then quarter. Cut each quarter into 4 or 6 pieces.

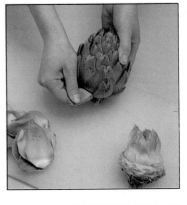

In a 12-inch skillet, melt butter. Add artichoke and sauté 2 to 3 minutes. Add a little water, cover, and simmer until tender. Uncover and boil to evaporate all water. Using a fork, in a bowl, lightly beat eggs with trout, chopped parsley, salt, and pepper until yolks and whites are blended.

Pour eggs into skillet. Reduce heat to very low. Cook about 15 minutes until mixture is almost set and top is still creamy and moist. Meanwhile, preheat broiler. Place pan under broiler 30 to 60 seconds until frittata is just set. Using a spatula, loosen edges, then slide it onto a warm place. Serve in wedges with a green salad, garnished with lemon wedges and sprigs of parsley.

Makes 4 servings.

MIXED FISH STEW

1 red snapper, bream, or trout, about 12 ounces
1 (6-oz.) piece sea bass
1 (12-oz.) monkfish fillet
1/2 bay leaf
1-1/2 tablespoons olive oil
1 (4-oz.) fennel bulb
8 ounces small carrots
2/3 cup thinly sliced onion
1 small garlic clove, finely crushed
Pinch of saffron threads, toasted and crushed
2/3 cup dry white wine
5 tablespoons half-and-half
Salt and pepper
1/2 bunch green onions, cut diagonally into thin strips
Dill sprigs to garnish

Cut whole fish into thick slices. Place head and tail into a small saucepan. Remove skin and bones from bass and add them to pan.

Trim fine skin from monkfish and add skin to pan with bay leaf and 2/3 cup water. Simmer 20 minutes, then strain and reserve the stock. Thickly slice raw bass and monkfish.

In a Dutch oven, heat oil. Cut fennel and carrots into thin strips and add to casserole with onion, garlic, and saffron. Cook 3 to 4 minutes. Add 4 tablespoons wine, then boil until most of liquid has evaporated. Add remaining wine and boil until reduced by half.

Stir in reserved stock, 2-1/2 tablespoons half-and-half, and monkfish, then season with salt and pepper. Cover and simmer 10 minutes.

Add snapper and bass, cover, and cook 10 minutes longer or until fish is just cooked. Gently stir in remaining half-and-half and scatter green onions over the top. Serve garnished with sprigs of dill.

Makes 4 servings.

SALMON WITH AVOCADO SALSA

4 salmon fillets with skin, about 6 ounces each
2-1/2 tablespoons olive oil
Sea salt and pepper
Lime wedges and cilantro leaves to garnish
SALSA:
1 ripe but firm avocado
2 large ripe tomatoes, peeled, seeded, and finely
   chopped
1/2 small red onion, finely chopped
1/2 to 1 fresh red chile, seeded and thinly sliced
1 garlic clove, finely chopped
2 tablespoons lime juice
2 tablespoons chopped fresh cilantro
Salt and pepper

To make salsa, halve avocado, then discard seed, quarter each half, and remove skin. Dice avocado flesh, and in a bowl mix with remaining salsa ingredients. Cover and refrigerate about 1 hour.

Pat fish dry with paper towels, then brush skin with some of the olive oil. In a heavy skillet, heat remaining oil until hot. Add salmon, skin sides down, and cook 10 to 15 minutes depending on thickness of fillets, until skin is quite crisp, sides are opaque, and top is slightly soft as it should be rare. Season salmon with sea salt and pepper, garnish with lime wedges and cilantro leaves, and serve with salsa.

Makes 4 servings.

—SALMON WITH HERB SAUCE—

1/2 onion, chopped
1 carrot, chopped
1 stalk celery, chopped
1 lemon, sliced
1 (3-1/2-lb.) salmon
Bouquet garni of 2 bay leaves and sprig each rosemary,
    sage, and parsley
3/4 cup dry white wine
Salt and pepper
1 bunch watercress, roughly chopped
3 tablespoons chopped fresh parsley
2 tablespoons chopped fresh chervil
1 tablespoon chopped fresh dill
1 cup ricotta cheese or low-fat soft cheese
Lime and lemon slices and herb sprigs to garnish

Preheat oven to 435F (220C). Place a large piece of foil on a large baking sheet. Make a bed of all the vegetables and half the lemon slices on foil. Place salmon on vegetables and add bouquet garni and remaining lemon slices. Fold up foil. Pour in wine, season with salt and pepper, and seal edges of foil tightly. Bake 1 hour. Remove baking sheet from oven and cool fish in foil.

Strain cooking liquid, then boil it until reduced to about 1/3 cup. Add watercress and herbs and boil until softened. Pour herb mixture and liquid into a blender or food processor. Add cheese and puree. Season with salt and pepper. Pour into a serving bowl and refrigerate. Lift fish onto a rack. Carefully remove skin, fins, and fatty line that runs along spine. Transfer to a large serving plate, garnish with lime and lemon slices and sprigs of herbs and serve with sauce.

Makes 6 servings.

COULIBIAC

1/4 cup long-grain rice
Salt and pepper
12 ounces spinach, stems removed and torn
Pinch freshly grated nutmeg
6 tablespoons butter
1 onion, finely chopped
3/4 cup plus 2 tablespoons milk
1 pound salmon fillets
2 tablespoons all-purpose flour
1/4 cup sour cream
1-1/2 tablespoons chopped fresh parsley
1-1/2 tablespoons snipped fresh chives
2 hard-cooked eggs, coarsely chopped
4 large sheets phyllo pastry dough

In a saucepan, bring 2/3 cup water to a boil. Add rice and salt, stir, and then return to a boil. Cover and cook 12 to 15 minutes until rice is tender and water absorbed. Meanwhile, wash but do not dry spinach. Put spinach into a saucepan and heat until there is no visible liquid. Turn into a colander and press out excess liquid. Season with salt, pepper, and nutmeg. Let cool.

In a small pan, melt 2 tablespoons butter. Add onion and cook until softened but not browned. Stir into rice. Let cool. Pour milk into a shallow saucepan. Add salmon and bring to a boil, then poach 10 to 15 minutes or until only just cooked. Drain and reserve milk. Skin and flake fish.

In a saucepan, melt 2 tablespoons butter. Stir in flour; cook 1 minute, then slowly pour in reserved milk, stirring. Bring to a boil, stirring, and simmer about 4 minutes, stirring occasionally. Remove from heat. Let cool slightly, then fold in salmon, cream, herbs, eggs, salt, and pepper. Let cool completely.

Preheat oven to 400F (205C). Butter a baking sheet. In a saucepan, melt remaining butter. Cut phyllo pastry in half to make 8 sheets. Lay 1 sheet on baking sheet and brush lightly with melted butter, then repeat with 3 more sheets phyllo pastry; keep remaining phyllo pastry covered with damp cloth.

Spoon rice onto phyllo pastry, leaving a 1-inch border. Cover with spinach, then fish mixture. Lay a sheet of phyllo pastry over filling, brush with butter, then repeat with remaining phyllo pastry. Press edges together, then bake in the oven about 25 minutes or until pastry is crisp and golden.

Makes 4 to 6 servings.

SALMON STIR-FRY

1 pound small asparagus, trimmed
2 tablespoons peanut oil
10 ounces salmon, skinned, boned, and cut into thin
    strips 1 inch long
Squeeze of lemon juice
1 tablespoon soy sauce
2 teaspoons sesame oil
Salt and pepper
Lightly toasted sesame seeds to garnish
Chinese egg noodles to serve

Slice asparagus diagonally into 1/2-inch pieces. Bring a saucepan of salted water to a boil. Add asparagus and cook 1-1/2 minutes. Drain and rinse.

In a wok or large skillet, heat peanut oil. Add asparagus and stir-fry 1-1/2 minutes.

Add salmon, lemon juice, soy sauce, and sesame oil. Stir-fry 2 minutes. Add pepper and a little salt. Serve immediately, sprinkled with sesame seeds, accompanied by egg noodles.

Makes 4 servings.

CHINESE SALAD WITH SALMON

12 ounces Chinese noodles
1 tablespoon salted black beans, coarsely chopped
3 ounces bean sprouts
1 tablespoon peanut oil
1 pound salmon fillets, cut into 1-inch cubes
2 teaspoons grated gingerroot
2 tablespoons rice wine or medium-dry sherry
2 teaspoons sesame oil
3 ounces watercress leaves and fine stems
1/2 red bell pepper, seeded and chopped

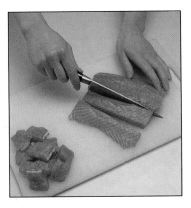

Cook noodles according to package directions, drain, and rinse well with cold water. Drain again, then put into a serving bowl, cover and refrigerate while preparing remaining ingredients. Soak black beans in 1 to 2 tablespoons hot water. Bring a pan of water to a boil, add bean sprouts and boil 1 minute. Drain, rinse under cold running water, then set aside. In a skillet, heat peanut oil. Add salmon, in batches if necessary, and fry until just cooked and pale gold. Drain on paper towels.

Add gingerroot, rice wine or sherry, sesame oil, and half the watercress. Boil a few seconds, then add black beans and remove from heat. Add bean sprouts, bell pepper, and salmon to noodles. Pour warm dressing over noodle mixture and garnish with remaining watercress.

Makes 4 servings.

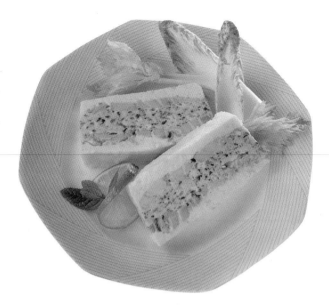

LAYERED FISH TERRINE

1 pound salmon, skinned and boned
Salt and white pepper
2/3 cup medium-dry white wine
2 small bunches watercress, trimmed
1 tablespoon butter
1 shallot, finely chopped
1 pound firm white fish, such as hake, monkfish, or
    cod, skinned, boned, and cubed
2 egg whites
1 cup whipping cream, chilled
Lime slices and mint sprigs to garnish

Cut salmon into long strips. Put salmon strips
into a dish. Season with salt and white pepper
and pour wine over salmon. Cover and
refrigerate about 1 hour.

Meanwhile, bring a saucepan of lightly salted
water to a boil. Add watercress and blanch 1
minute. Drain watercress, rinse under cold
running water, and drain again. Dry on paper
towels; set aside.

In a small saucepan, melt butter. Add shallot and cook over low heat until softened but not browned. In a blender or food processor, puree shallot with fish. Add egg whites and season with salt and pepper. Process 1 minute, then, with motor running, slowly pour in cream. Remove and reserve two-thirds of fish mixture. Add watercress to blender or food processor and puree briefly. Chill both mixtures 30 minutes.

Preheat oven to 350F (175C). Lightly oil a 10" × 3-1/2" terrine pan. Spread half the plain fish mixture in the bottom of the pan, then half the salmon strips followed by all the green mixture. Cover this with remaining salmon strips, then remaining white mixture.

Cover terrine with foil. In a roasting pan, place terrine and pour in enough boiling water to come halfway up sides of terrine. Bake about 40 minutes until a skewer inserted in center comes out clean. Transfer terrine to a wire rack to cool slightly, then refrigerate. Cut into slices and serve garnished with lime slices and sprigs of mint.

Makes 4 to 6 servings.

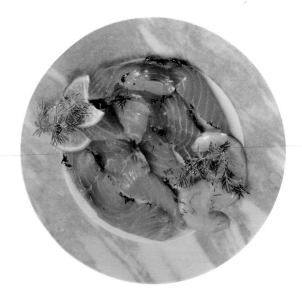

GRAVLAX

3 tablespoons sea salt
2 to 3 teaspoons light brown sugar
2 teaspoons crushed black peppercorns
6 tablespoons lime juice
Large bunch dill
1 (3- to 4-lb.) salmon, filleted, with skin
Lime slices and dill sprigs to garnish
DILL & MUSTARD SAUCE:
3 tablespoons Dijon mustard
2 tablespoons white-wine vinegar
1 tablespoon sugar
2/3 cup grapeseed oil
2 tablespoons finely chopped fresh dill
Salt and pepper

In a small bowl, mix together sea salt, sugar, peppercorns, and lime juice. In a shallow, nonmetallic dish, spread some dill. Add one-quarter of salt mixture. Lay one salmon fillet, skin side down, in dish. Cover with plenty of dill and sprinkle with half remaining salt mixture. Place remaining salmon on top, skin side up. Cover salmon with remaining dill and sprinkle with remaining salt mixture. Cover with parchment paper, then plastic wrap.

Place a 2-pound weight on top and refrigerate 3 days, turning occasionally and spooning liquid back between fillets occasionally. To make sauce, in a bowl, mix together mustard, vinegar, and sugar, then gradually beat in oil. Add chopped dill, salt, and pepper. Drain salmon well, pat dry, and trim off any hard edges. Very thinly slice salmon on the diagonal, discarding skin. Garnish with lime slices and sprigs of dill and serve with sauce.

Makes 8 servings.

── TUNA PEPERONATA ──

6 slices tuna, about 1 inch thick each
4 garlic cloves
1/3 cup olive oil
1 large onion, finely chopped
1 large red bell pepper, thinly sliced
1 green bell pepper, thinly sliced
14 ounces tomatoes, peeled, seeded, and diced
1 tablespoon sun-dried tomato paste
3 sprigs thyme
1 bay leaf
Salt and pepper
Parsley sprigs to garnish

Cut slits in tuna. Cut 2 garlic cloves into slivers and insert in slits in tuna. In a large skillet, heat half the oil. Add tuna and cook until lightly browned on both sides. Remove tuna from skillet and set aside. In skillet, heat remaining oil. Add onion and bell peppers and cook over medium heat, stirring frequently, about 10 minutes or until soft.

Chop remaining garlic. Add to pan and cook 1 minute, then add tomatoes, tomato paste, thyme, and bay leaf. Simmer, uncovered, 15 to 20 minutes, stirring occasionally. Return tuna to pan and season with salt and pepper. Cover with buttered parchment paper and simmer 15 minutes. Serve garnished with sprigs of parsley.

Makes 6 servings.

WARM TUNA NICOISE

1-1/2 pounds small new potatoes
Pepper
1 pound green beans
2 tablespoons olive oil
4 tuna steaks, about 5 ounces each and 1/2 inch thick
2 tomatoes, chopped
Nicoise or small ripe oil-cured olives to garnish
DRESSING:
2 teaspoons whole-grain mustard
1 tablespoon anchovy paste
1 garlic clove, finely chopped
3 tablespoons red-wine vinegar
1/4 cup olive oil
2 teaspoons capers, drained

To make dressing, in a blender, process mustard, anchovy paste, garlic, and vinegar together. With motor running, slowly pour in oil. Stir in capers and set aside.

In a pan of boiling water, boil potatoes in their skins until tender. Drain well. Cut potatoes into 3/4-inch pieces. Put potatoes into a bowl. Season with pepper. Stir 3 tablespoons of dressing into potatoes.

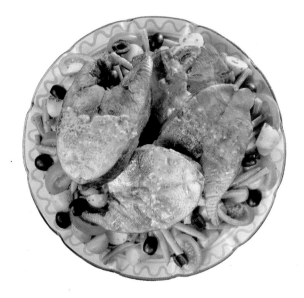

Meanwhile, cut beans into 1-inch pieces. Heat a large, heavy skillet. Add 1 tablespoon oil, then beans (be careful to not splatter). Stir-fry about 5 minutes until tender but still crisp. Transfer beans to a separate bowl. Stir in 1 tablespoon dressing.

To skillet, add remaining oil. Season both sides of tuna with pepper, then add to pan, and cook over medium-high heat, about 4 minutes, turning once, until brown outside and still slightly rare in the middle.

Transfer tuna to a warm serving dish. Add tomatoes to dish with tuna. Drizzle 1 table-spoon dressing over tomatoes; drizzle remaining dressing over tuna. Add beans and potatoes and scatter olives over them. Serve immediately.

Makes 4 servings.

-TUNA & GINGER VINAIGRETTE-

1 (1-inch) piece gingerroot, finely chopped
2 large green onions, white and some green parts thinly
    sliced
1 cup olive oil
Juice of 2 limes
2 tablespoons soy sauce
2 tablespoons sesame oil
1 bunch cilantro, finely chopped
Pepper
6 tuna steaks, 5 to 6 ounces each
Leeks and red bell peppers stir-fried with sesame seeds
Cilantro sprigs to garnish

Preheat broiler. To make vinaigrette, in a
bowl, stir together gingerroot, green onions,
olive oil, lime juice, and soy sauce. Beat in
sesame oil. Add chopped cilantro and season
with pepper. Set aside.

Place tuna on a broiler pan. Broil tuna 3-1/2
to 4 minutes on each side, or a little longer for
well-done fish. Spoon some dressing onto 6
serving plates. Add tuna. Serve with leeks
and red bell peppers, garnished with sprigs
of cilantro. Serve any remaining dressing
separately.

Makes 6 servings.

HERRINGS IN OATS

About 1 tablespoon Dijon mustard
About 1-1/2 teaspoons tarragon vinegar
1/3 cup mayonnaise
1/3 cup plain yogurt
4 herrings, about 8 ounces each, cleaned and heads and
    tails removed
Salt and pepper
1 lemon, halved
2/3 cup steel-cut oats
Rice and artichoke heart salad to serve
Lemon wedges and cilantro sprigs to garnish

In a small bowl, beat mustard and vinegar to taste into mayonnaise and yogurt. Spoon into a small serving bowl and chill.

Preheat broiler. Working with 1 fish at a time, place fish on a board, cut-side down and open out. Press gently along backbone with your thumbs. Turn fish over and carefully lift away backbone and attached bones.

Season with salt and pepper and squeeze lemon juice over both sides of fish. Fold fish in half, skin side outward. Repeat with remaining fish. Coat each fish evenly in oats, pressing in well but gently. Place herrings on a broiler pan. Broil herrings 3 to 4 minutes on each side until brown and crisp and flesh flakes easily. Serve hot with the mustard sauce, accompanied by salad and garnished with lemon wedges and sprigs of cilantro.

Makes 4 servings.

— MACKEREL WITH MUSTARD —

2 tablespoons Dijon mustard
1/4 cup finely chopped fresh cilantro
2 garlic cloves, finely crushed
2 to 3 teaspoons lemon juice
Salt and pepper
4 mackerel, about 10 ounces each
Rolled oats
Tomato, fennel, and thyme salad to serve
Lemon wedges and cilantro sprigs to garnish

Preheat broiler. In a bowl, mix together mustard, cilantro, garlic, and lemon juice. Season with salt and pepper.

Using the point of a sharp knife, cut 3 slashes on each side of each mackerel. Spoon mustard mixture into slashes and sprinkle with a little oats. Wrap each fish in a large piece of foil and fold edges of foil together to seal tightly.

Place foil packages under hot broiler 5 minutes. Open foil, turn fish, reseal packages, and broil 2 to 3 minutes longer. Open foil, place fish under the broiler and broil 2 to 3 minutes or until cooked through and flesh flakes easily. Serve with a salad, garnished with lemon wedges and sprigs of cilantro.

Makes 4 servings.

– MACKEREL WITH CUCUMBERS –

1/2 cucumber, peeled
Salt and pepper
3/4 cup plain yogurt
1-1/4 tablespoons chopped fresh mint
1 garlic clove, finely crushed
1/2 teaspoon harissa or pinch chile powder
2 teaspoons ground cumin
2 tablespoons light olive oil
Squeeze lemon juice
4 mackerel, cleaned
Red Belgian endive, bean, and yellow bell pepper salad
   to serve

Halve cucumber lengthwise, scoop out seeds, and thinly slice.

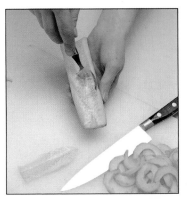

In a colander, spread out cucumber, sprinkle with salt, and let drain 30 minutes. Rinse cucumber, and dry with paper towels. In a bowl, put cucumber with yogurt and mint. Cover and chill 2 hours. In a mortar or small bowl, put garlic, pound in harissa or chile powder, and cumin using a pestle or end of a rolling pin. Add lemon juice and season with salt and pepper.

With the point of a sharp knife, cut 2 slashes in each side of each fish. Spread spice mixture over the fish and let marinate 15 to 30 minutes. Preheat broiler. Broil fish 7 to 8 minutes on each side. Serve with cucumber mixture, accompanied by red Belgian endive, bean, and yellow bell pepper salad.

Makes 4 servings.

-SARDINES IN CILANTRO SAUCE-

2 pounds sardines (at least 12)
1/4 cup olive oil
Grated peel of 1-1/2 limes
1-1/2 tablespoons lime juice
3/4 teaspoon coriander seeds, toasted and finely
   crushed
3 tablespoons chopped fresh cilantro
Salt and pepper
Cilantro sprigs to garnish
Lime wedges to serve

Into a shallow, nonmetallic dish, put sardines. In a bowl, beat together oil, lime peel and juice, coriander seeds, chopped cilantro, salt, and pepper.

Pour cilantro mixture over sardines and let marinate 1 hour, turning sardines over once.

Preheat broiler. Remove sardines from dish and broil 4 to 5 minutes on each side, basting with cilantro mixture. Serve sardines garnished with sprigs of cilantro and accompanied by lime wedges.

Makes 4 servings.

STUFFED SARDINES

12 sardines, cleaned
1 tablespoon each chopped fresh parsley, chives, dill,
    and basil and 2 small sage leaves
1 clove garlic
2 tablespoons pine nuts, lightly toasted
Pinch crushed dried chiles
2 tablespoons light olive oil
Salt and pepper
1/2 lemon
2-1/2 tablespoons fresh bread crumbs
Grilled baby vegetables and lemon wedges to serve

Preheat oven to 425F (220C). Oil a wide, shallow baking dish. Cut heads and tails off sardines.

Using a thin, sharp knife, slit along underside of bodies to open them out. Discard intestines. Wash cavities of fish, then pat dry with paper towels. Working with one fish at a time, lay fish, skin side up, on a work surface. Using your thumbs, press gently along center of the back to dislodge backbone. Turn fish over and gently pull away backbone and any attached bones. Repeat with remaining sardines.

Finely chop herbs, garlic, and nuts. In a bowl, mix with chiles, 1 tablespoon oil, salt, and pepper. In dish, lay 6 sardines, skin sides down, in a single layer. Squeeze some lemon juice over, then spread some herb mixture on each fish. Cover with remaining sardines, skin sides up. Sprinkle with bread crumbs, then trickle remaining oil over the top. Bake about 10 minutes until golden. Serve hot or at room temperature with baby vegetables and lemon wedges.

Makes 4 servings.

—JOHN DORY WITH ORANGE—

4 John Dory fillets, about 5-1/2 ounces each
4 sprigs mint
1/4 cup dry white vermouth
Finely grated peel and juice of 1 orange
1 to 2 tablespoons virgin olive oil
Salt and pepper
Orange slices to garnish

Preheat oven to 350F (175C). Cut 4 pieces aluminum foil each large enough to enclose one piece of fish. Oil top side of each piece. Place one fish in center of each piece of foil.

Pinch out center of each mint sprig and reserve for garnish. Finely chop remaining mint, then, in a bowl, mix together with vermouth, orange peel and juice, olive oil, salt, and pepper.

Fold up sides of foil, spoon one-quarter of orange mixture over each fish. Seal edges of foil tightly. Place foil packages on a baking sheet. Bake 12 to 15 minutes. Serve garnished with orange slices and reserved mint sprigs.

Makes 4 servings.

—FISH & WATERCRESS SAUCE—

4 John Dory or brill fillets, about 6 ounces each,
   skinned
Mixed salad to serve
SAUCE:
2 tablespoons unsalted butter
Leaves and fine stems of 1 large bunch watercress
2/3 cup mayonnaise
About 1 tablespoon lemon juice
Salt and pepper

Bring water in bottom of steamer to a boil. In
a steaming basket, lay fish fillets in a single
layer. Cover basket, then place over steamer
base and steam about 5 minutes.

Meanwhile, to make sauce, in a skillet, melt
butter. Add watercress and sauté 2 to 3
minutes.

To a blender or food processor, transfer
watercress and butter. Add mayonnaise and
mix briefly. With motor running, slowly
trickle in 1 tablespoon lemon juice. Season
with salt and pepper and add extra lemon
juice if necessary. Season fish and serve with
mixed salad, accompanied by watercress
sauce.

Makes 4 servings.

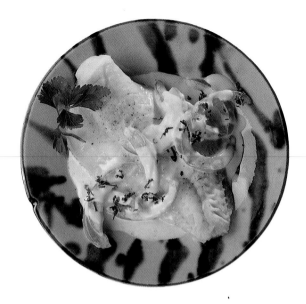

PORGY DUGLERE

Salt and pepper
4 porgy or red bream fillets, about 6 ounces each
1 cup fish stock
6 tablespoons medium-dry white wine
2/3 cup heavy cream
1 large sun-ripened beefsteak tomato, peeled, seeded,
   and cut into 1/2-inch strips
Basil or parsley sprigs to garnish

Season fish. In a well-buttered skillet, place fish in a single layer. Add stock and wine. Bring just to a boil. Reduce heat, cover pan, and poach fish 4 to 6 minutes.

Using a pancake turner, transfer fish to a warm plate, cover, and keep warm. Boil cooking liquid rapidly until reduced to one-quarter. Stir cream into pan and simmer 2 to 3 minutes.

Add tomato strips and heat gently 1 minute. Season sauce, then pour it over fish. Serve garnished with basil or parsley sprigs.

Makes 4 servings.

—BAKED PORGY WITH FENNEL—

2 fennel bulbs, thinly sliced
1 red onion, thinly sliced
3 garlic cloves, sliced
1 lemon, peeled and thinly sliced
3 small sprigs rosemary
2 porgy, scup, or red bream, about 1-1/4 pounds each,
  cleaned and scaled
1 tablespoon fennel seeds, cracked
Salt and pepper
5 tablespoons olive oil
Rosemary sprigs to garnish

Preheat oven to 350F (175C). In a baking dish large enough to hold fish, spread fennel, onion, garlic, lemon, and rosemary evenly.

Cook in oven about 8 minutes. Meanwhile, with the point of a sharp knife, cut 2 slashes in each side of each fish. Put half the fennel seeds inside each fish.

Place fish on vegetables. Season with salt and pepper and pour oil over them. Bake 20 to 25 minutes, turning fish halfway through, until vegetables and fish are tender. Serve garnished with rosemary sprigs.

Makes 4 to 6 servings.

– PORGY WITH LEMON & HERBS –

2 tablespoons chopped fresh mixed herbs, such as
   thyme, rosemary, marjoram, fennel, and basil
1/2 clove garlic, chopped
Juice of 1/2 lemon
Salt and pepper
3 tablespoons extra-virgin olive oil
4 porgy, scup, or red bream fillets, about 9 ounces each
Finely grated lemon peel and slices and parsley sprigs
   to garnish

Preheat oven to 400F (205C). Chop together
herbs and garlic. Into a bowl, put chopped
herbs and garlic. Stir in lemon juice and
season with salt and pepper. Using a fork,
gradually beat in olive.

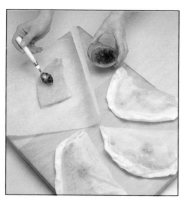

Cut 4 pieces of parchment paper or foil so
each is large enough to enclose a fish. Place
one fish on each piece of paper and spoon
herb mixture over. Fold paper or foil loosely
over fish and seal edges tightly.

Place paper or foil packages on a baking
sheet. Cook in oven about 15 minutes. Serve
fish in the paper or foil packages garnished
with lemon peel and slices and parsley sprigs.

Makes 4 servings.

CHINESE-STYLE PORGY

1/4 cup soy sauce
1 carrot, cut into fine strips
3 green onions, cut into fine strips
1 (1-inch) piece fresh gingerroot, finely shredded
1-1/2 pounds porgy, scup, or red bream fillets
2 tablespoons sesame oil
2 tablespoons peanut oil
1 fresh red chile, cut into rings and seeded
1 clove garlic, shredded
Fresh snipped chives to garnish

On a large serving plate, put a little of the soy sauce.

In a bowl, mix together carrot, green onions, and ginger. Use half to make a bed on heat-proof plate for fish that will fit in a steaming basket. Place fish on vegetables. Scatter remaining vegetables over, then trickle remaining soy sauce over. Place plate in steaming basket and cover basket. Fill bottom of steamer with water and bring to a boil. Put basket on steamer and cook 10 to 14 minutes until flesh flakes easily.

Meanwhile, in a small saucepan, very gently heat sesame and peanut oils. Add chile and garlic, then cook 5 to 7 minutes. Remove plate from steaming basket and baste fish with cooking juices. Pour hot oil, garlic, and chile over. Serve garnished with snipped chives.

Makes 2 servings.

—FISH PLAKI—

about 2-1/2 pounds fish, such as porgy, sea bass, gray
   mullet, red snapper, or pompano, scaled
Juice of 1/2 lemon
2 tablespoons olive oil
1 onion, chopped
1 carrot, finely chopped
1 stalk celery, chopped
2 garlic cloves, chopped
1 teaspoon coriander seeds, crushed
1 pound tomatoes, peeled, seeded, and chopped
3 sun-dried tomato halves, finely chopped
1/3 cup dry white wine
Leaves from bunch parsley, finely chopped
Salt and pepper
Parsley sprigs to garnish

Preheat oven to 375F (190C). Into a baking
dish, put fish. Squeeze lemon juice over. In a
saucepan heat oil. Add onion, carrot, and
celery and cook, stirring occasionally, until
onion has softened but not colored. Stir in
garlic and cook about 3 minutes longer. Stir
in coriander seeds, tomatoes, sun-dried
tomatoes, wine, and parsley. Season with salt
and pepper and simmer a few minutes until
well blended.

Using a pancake turner, lift fish and pour
about one-quarter of the tomato mixture
underneath. Lay fish down again and pour
remaining tomato mixture over. Cover dish
and bake in the oven about 40 minutes. Serve
garnished with parsley sprigs.

Makes 4 servings.

-SKATE WITH ANCHOVY SAUCE-

4 small skate wings
Salt and pepper
1 tablespoon olive oil
1 tablespoon unsalted butter
Sugar snap peas and new potatoes to serve
Basil sprigs to garnish
SAUCE:
1 large clove garlic
6 anchovy fillets, chopped
2-1/2 tablespoons capers
2-1/2 teaspoons whole-grain mustard
1-1/2 tablespoons chopped fresh basil
3 tablespoons chopped fresh parsley
3 tablespoons lime juice
3 tablespoons virgin olive oil
Black pepper

To make sauce, in a small bowl, crush garlic with anchovies. Stir in capers, mustard, basil, parsley, and lime juice, then gradually beat in oil. Season with black pepper and set aside.

Season skate wings. In a large nonstick skillet, heat oil and melt butter. Add 2 skate wings and fry about 4 minutes on each side until lightly browned. Transfer skate wings to paper towels, then fry remaining skate in same way. Return skate to pan, pour in sauce, and heat briefly until warmed through. Serve with sugar snap peas and new potatoes, garnished with sprigs of basil.

Makes 4 servings.

STIR-FRIED SQUID

2 pounds small squid
1-1/2 tablespoons peanut oil
2 garlic cloves, slivered
1 (1/2-inch) piece gingerroot, finely chopped
2 plump stalks lemon grass, finely crushed and chopped
4 green onions, white and some green parts sliced
1 tablespoon rice wine or medium-dry sherry
1 tablespoon chopped fresh parsley and basil
Parsley sprigs and lemon wedges to garnish

Hold head of each squid in turn just below the eyes and gently pull from body pouch; the soft innards, including ink sac, will come with it. Discard innards.

Pull back rim of body pouch to locate the clear, plastic-looking quill. Carefully pull out and discard. Cut head from tentacles just below eyes; discard head. Chop tentacles. Cut out small round of cartilage at base of tentacles. Squeeze beak-like mouth in center of tentacles to remove. Slip your fingers under skin of body pouch, peel off, then cut edible fins from body. Rinse squid under cold running water and dry well. Thinly slice squid.

In a wok or large skillet, heat oil. Add garlic, ginger, and lemon grass and stir-fry gently 1 minute. Increase heat, add squid and stir-fry 1 minute. Lower heat, add green onions and cook 1 minute longer. Add wine and heat briefly, then sprinkle with chopped parsley and basil. Garnish with parsley sprigs and lemon wedges. Serve.

Makes 4 servings.

STUFFED SQUID

about 12 small squid
1/4 cup olive oil
1 small onion, finely chopped
2 garlic cloves, chopped
4 green onions, chopped
4 anchovy fillets, chopped
6 tomatoes, peeled, seeded, and chopped
2 tablespoons chopped mixed herbs
2 tablespoons fresh bread crumbs
2 egg yolks, beaten
Salt and pepper
1 lemon, halved
Lemon and cucumber slices and chervil sprigs
    to garnish

Prepare squid as Stir-fried Squid (opposite) but do not slice bodies. In a skillet, heat 1 tablespoon oil. Add onion, garlic, green onions, and squid tentacles. Cook until onions are tender. Stir in anchovies, tomatoes, herbs, and bread crumbs. Cook, stirring, 1 minute longer, then remove from heat and stir in egg yolks. Season with plenty of pepper.

Preheat oven to 350F (175C). Oil a shallow baking dish. Divide herb mixture between squid bodies, taking care not to overfill them. Close openings with wooden picks. In prepared dish, place squid in a single layer. Squeeze lemon juice over squid, sprinkle with remaining oil, and season. Bake in the oven about 20 minutes until tender, basting with cooking juices occasionally. Serve garnished with lemon and cucumber slices and chervil sprigs.

Makes 4 servings.

– TURKISH SWORDFISH KABOBS –

1-1/4 pounds swordfish, cut into 1" × 1-1/2" cubes
Pasta to serve
Lime wedges and parsley sprigs to garnish
MARINADE:
1/4 cup lemon juice
1/4 cup olive oil
1 shallot, finely chopped
3 fresh bay leaves, torn
1-1/2 teaspoons paprika
Salt and pepper
LEMON SAUCE:
3 tablespoons olive oil
3 tablespoons lemon juice
3 tablespoons chopped fresh parsley

To prepare marinade, in a small bowl, mix ingredients together. In a wide, shallow, nonmetallic dish, lay swordfish cubes in a single layer. Pour marinade over and turn fish so it is evenly coated. Cover and refrigerate 4 to 5 hours, turning fish occasionally.

In a bowl, mix together sauce ingredients. Season with salt and pepper; set aside. Preheat broiler or barbecue. Oil broiler tray or grill rack. Remove fish from marinade and thread onto 4 kabob skewers. Broil or barbecue fish 4 to 5 minutes each side, basting frequently. Serve with sauce on a bed of pasta, garnished with lime wedges and sprigs of parsley.

Makes 4 servings.

— SWORDFISH WITH TOMATOES —

3 tablespoons olive oil
4 swordfish steaks
1 small onion, finely chopped
2 garlic cloves, crushed
1-1/4 pounds tomatoe, skinned, seeded, and chopped
2 sun-dried tomato halves, finely chopped
2 tablespoons chopped fresh parsley
1 bay leaf, torn
Pepper
8 oil-cured ripe olives, halved and pitted
Rice and zucchini batons to serve
Basil sprigs to garnish

In a skillet, heat half the oil. Add fish and cook quickly to brown on both sides.

Transfer fish to a plate. In pan, heat remaining oil. Add onion and garlic and cook until softened but not colored. Stir in chopped tomatoes, sun-dried tomatoes, chopped parsley, and bay leaf. Stir-fry about 1 minute, then boil until thickened.

Season tomato mixture with pepper. Add fish and baste with sauce. Cook gently, turning fish once, 10 to 15 minutes until fish is cooked through and flakes easily. Just before the end of the cooking time, scatter pitted olives over top. Serve with rice and zucchini batons, garnished with sprigs of basil.

Makes 4 servings.

ESCABECHE

6 to 8 red snapper or catfish fillets, cleaned and scaled
3 tablespoons seasoned flour
3 tablespoons olive oil
2 to 3 tablespoons chopped fresh cilantro
MARINADE:
Large pinch saffron threads, toasted
2 tablespoons olive oil
2 red onions, thinly sliced
2 red bell peppers, seeded and sliced
1/2 teaspoon dried chile flakes
1-1/2 teaspoons cumin seeds, lightly crushed
Finely grated peel and juice of 1 orange
2 to 3 tablespoons rice vinegar
Pinch sugar
Salt and pepper

To make marinade, crush saffron. In a bowl, soak in warm water 10 minutes. In a skillet, heat oil. Gently cook onions 2 minutes. Add bell peppers, chile flakes, and cumin. Fry until vegetables are soft. Stir in saffron and liquid, orange peel and juice, vinegar, sugar, salt, and pepper. Bubble a few minutes, then set aside and let cool.

Toss fish in flour. In a skillet, heat 3 table-spoons oil. Add fish and fry 2 to 3 minutes on each side until just cooked through and browned. In a shallow, nonmetallic dish, place fish in a single layer. Pour marinade over it. Cover and refrigerate 4 to 12 hours. Return to room temperature 15 minutes before serving. Stir in cilantro.

Serves 6 to 8 as an appetizer.

Note: Garnish with orange slices and sprigs of cilantro, if wished.

—CAJUN-STYLE RED SNAPPER—

2 red snapper, 1-1/4 to 1-1/2 pounds each
2 tablespoons unsalted butter
2 tablespoons olive oil
SPICE MIX:
1 plump clove garlic
1/2 onion
1 teaspoon salt
1 teaspoon paprika
1/2 teaspoon red (cayenne) pepper
1/2 teaspoon ground cumin
1/2 teaspoon mustard powder
1 teaspoon each dried thyme and dried oregano
1/2 teaspoon pepper

With the point of a sharp knife, cut 3 slashes on each side of both fish.

To make spice mix, in a pestle and mortar or in a bowl using the end of a rolling pin, crush together garlic and onion with salt. Stir in remaining spice mix ingredients. Spread some spice mix over each fish, making sure it goes into the slashes. In a shallow dish, lay fish. Cover and refrigerate 1 hour.

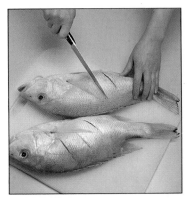

In a large skillet, melt butter and heat oil until sizzling. Add fish and fry about 4 minutes on each side until fish is cooked through and flakes easily and spice coating has blackened.

Makes 2 servings.

Note: Serve with a colorful selection of tomato, lemon, and lime slices with thyme and parsley sprigs.

—RED SNAPPER & MUSHROOMS—

3 cups sliced mushrooms
4 green onions, green and white parts finely chopped
3-pound red snapper or grouper, cleaned and scaled but
    with head and tail left on
2-1/2 tablespoons chopped fresh cilantro
1 tablespoon olive oil
1 tablespoon butter, melted
2 tablespoons lemon juice
1-1/4 cups medium-dry white wine
2/3 cup freshly squeezed tangerine juice
Salt and pepper
Tangerine wedges to garnish

Preheat oven to 400F (205C). Butter a baking dish just large enough to hold the fish. In bottom of dish, scatter mushrooms and green onions. Place fish on top.

Sprinkle chopped cilantro over fish. In a bowl, mix together oil, butter, lemon juice, wine, and tangerine juice. Season with salt and pepper. Pour mixture over fish. Bake in oven 20 to 30 minutes until flesh flakes. If cooking juices are too thin, transfer fish and mushrooms to a warm serving plate and keep warm. Into a saucepan and boil to concentrate slightly, then pour over fish. Serve garnished with tangerine wedges.

Makes 4 servings.

──SWORDFISH WITH SAUCE──

3-1/2 tablespoons olive oil
1 clove garlic, finely chopped
2 cups diced zucchini
10 basil leaves
2 tablespoons fish stock or dry white wine
2 swordfish steaks, halved, or 4 mahi mahi (dolphin fish) fillets
1 large tomato, peeled, seeded, and chopped
Salt and pepper
Rice to serve
Basil sprigs to garnish

In a skillet, heat 1-1/2 tablespoons of the olive oil. Add garlic and cook gently until golden. Add zucchini and stock or wine.

Place fish on zucchini and put basil leaves and tomato on top of fish. Cover pan tightly and cook gently about 10 minutes. Transfer fish, with tomato, to warm plates. Season with salt and pepper, cover, and keep warm. If necessary, continue to cook zucchini until tender.

In a blender or food processor, puree zucchini, basil, and garlic. Slowly pour in 1 to 2 tablespoons oil and sufficient cooking water to make a soft puree. Season. Add zucchini puree to plate with fish. Serve with rice, garnished with sprigs of basil.

Makes 4 servings.

CANTONESE SHRIMP

1 orange
2 tablespoons soy sauce
2 tablespoons honey
2 tablespoons dry sherry
2 tablespoons white-wine vinegar
1 teaspoon Chinese five-spice powder
1-1/2 pounds raw jumbo shrimp
Green onions to garnish

With a vegetable peeler or small sharp knife, remove 6 strips of peel from orange, taking care not to include any white pith.

Cut strips into fine shreds. Bring a small saucepan of water to a boil. Add orange-peel strips and blanch 2 minutes. Drain peel. Into the empty pan, put orange-peel strips, soy sauce, honey, sherry, vinegar, and five-spice powder. Squeeze in juice from orange. Simmer 3 to 4 minutes, then leave to cool.

Place shrimp in a shallow dish, pour soy mixture over, and let stand 1 hour. In a skillet, stir-fry shrimp in the sauce 2 to 4 minutes until shrimp are pink and fully cooked. Serve garnished with green onions.

Makes 4 to 6 servings.

Variation: Use pomfret or pompano instead of shrimp.

—SHRIMP WITH ASIAN SAUCE—

1-1/2 pounds raw jumbo shrimp
Lime wedges and basil sprigs to garnish
MARINADE:
Handful Thai or ordinary fresh basil, finely chopped
2 tablespoons finely chopped garlic
2 tablespoons finely chopped fresh ginger root
2 tablespoons finely chopped green chiles
2 teaspoons rice wine or medium-dry sherry
2-1/2 tablespoons peanut oil
1 teaspoon Chinese sesame oil
Salt and pepper

To make marinade, in a pestle or a small bowl, pound ingredients together using a mortar or end of a rolling pin.

Discard legs and heads from shrimp. Using strong scissors, cut shrimp lengthwise in half, leaving tail end intact. Remove dark intestinal vein. Rub marinade over shrimp, spoon any remaining marinade over them, cover, and refrigerate 1 hour.

Preheat broiler or barbecue. Cook shrimp in a single layer about 3 minutes until curled and bright pink. Garnish with lime wedges and sprigs of basil. Serve any remaining marinade separately.

Makes 4 to 6 servings.

—BAKED SHRIMP & ZUCCHINI—

3 zucchini, thinly sliced lengthwise
1 cup crumbled bread, crusts removed
Small handful parsley, thyme, oregano, and mint,
    chopped together
2-1/2 tablespoons freshly grated Parmesan cheese
Pinch chili powder
Salt
12 raw jumbo shrimp, shelled with dark vein removed
3 to 4 tablespoons olive oil
Lemon and lime wedges and oregano sprigs to garnish

Preheat oven to 400F (205C). Oil 4 large, individual ovenproof dishes. Steam zucchini slices 2 minutes.

In a small bowl, mix together bread crumbs, herbs, cheese, chili powder, and a little salt. In bottom of each dish, place a layer of zucchini slices. Sprinkle with half the bread mixture. Arrange 3 shrimp in each dish, scatter some of the bread mixture over, and moisten with a little oil.

Cover with zucchini slices, then remaining bread mixture. Trickle a little oil over, then cover dishes tightly with foil. Pierce a few holes with a pick. Bake in oven 5 to 7 minutes. Serve garnished with lemon and lime wedges and sprigs of oregano.

Makes 4 servings.

—— INDIAN-STYLE SHRIMP ——

1-1/2 tablespoons oil
1 large onion, sliced
2 garlic cloves, crushed
1 to 2 green chiles, seeded and finely chopped
1 green bell pepper, seeded and finely chopped
1 (1/2-inch) piece fresh gingerroot, grated
1-1/4 teaspoons each cumin and coriander seeds,
    toasted and crushed
1 teaspoon ground cinnamon
Pinch saffron threads, toasted and crushed
Salt
1-1/2 pounds raw medium or large shrimp, shelled
1/2 cup plain yogurt
Rice to serve
Mint leaves and yogurt to garnish

In a nonstick pan, heat oil. Add onion, garlic, chiles and bell pepper. Cook fairly gently until softened and lightly browned. Stir in ginger, cumin, coriander, and cinnamon. Cook over slightly higher heat 1 to 2 minutes. Add saffron and salt, cover with water, then simmer, uncovered, 20 minutes, stirring occasionally. Add shrimp and more water, if necessary, to come halfway up shrimp. Cook gently about 4 minutes until shrimp turn pink.

Transfer shrimp to a warm plate. Boil cooking juices hard until they are syrupy. Stir a little of the juice into the yogurt, then stir back into pan. Heat through, stirring, but do not let boil. Add shrimp and turn them in the sauce. Serve with rice, garnished with mint and a swirl of yogurt.

Makes 4 servings.

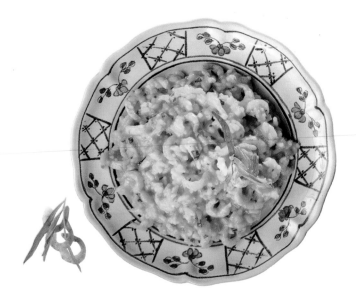

— SHRIMP RISOTTO —

1-1/4 pounds cooked shrimp or small shrimp with
  shells
Bouquet garni
5 black peppercorns
1 clove garlic, crushed
1/2 onion stuck with 1 clove
1-1/4 cups medium-dry white wine
5 tablespoons unsalted butter
2 shallots, finely chopped
Pinch saffron threads, toasted and crushed
1-1/2 cups arborio (Italian risotto) rice
2 tablespoons chopped fresh tarragon
Salt and pepper

Shell shrimp and set aside.

In a saucepan, put shrimp shells, bouquet
garni, peppercorns, garlic, onion, wine, and
4-1/2 cups water. Bring to a boil and simmer
20 minutes. Strain, pressing hard on shells.
Measure 5 cups stock; make up with water if
necessary. Bring to a boil.

In a heavy-bottomed saucepan, melt half the
butter. Cook shallots until translucent.
Using a wooden spoon, stir in saffron and
rice. Cook, stirring, 1 to 2 minutes until rice
is well coated and has absorbed butter.

Over medium heat, stir in about 2/3 cup boiling stock and continue to cook at a steady, but not too violent, bubble, stirring constantly, until no liquid is left. Stir in 2/3 cup boiling stock.

Continue to cook risotto, gradually adding smaller amounts of stock until rice is soft outside but is firm within, creamy, and bound together, neither moist nor dry; 15 to 20 minutes altogether. Add shrimp toward end of cooking time.

Remove pan from the heat. Dice remaining butter and stir in with tarragon. Cover and leave 1 minute for butter to be absorbed. Stir, taste, and add salt, if necessary, then serve immediately.

Makes 4 servings.

Note: Garnish with sprigs of tarragon, if wished.

SCALLOP, SHRIMP, & MINT SALAD

1/2 cup dry white wine
1/2 onion, chopped
1 bay leaf
4 black peppercorns, crushed
1 pound small zucchini
1 pound shelled scallops
1 pound raw large shrimp, shelled
2 tomatoes, peeled, seeded, and chopped
About 18 small mint leaves
DRESSING:
3 to 4 tablespoons lime juice
1/2 teaspoon finely grated lime peel
1/2 clove garlic, finely chopped
1/2 cup extra-virgin olive oil
2 tablespoons chopped fresh parsley
Salt and pepper

In a saucepan, heat together wine, onion, bay leaf, and peppercorns with 2-1/4 cups water. Simmer 15 minutes, then add zucchini and cook about 8 minutes longer until tender but still crisp. Using a slotted spoon, remove zucchini and drain on paper towels. Add scallops and shrimp to pan and poach until scallops just turn opaque, about 2 minutes, and shrimp become pink, 3 to 4 minutes.

Drain seafood and cool under cold running water. Halve scallops horizontally. Cut zucchini into thin strips. Into a serving dish, put zucchini, with seafood, tomatoes, and mint. To make dressing, in a small bowl, whisk ingredients together. Pour over salad and toss gently. Cover and chill 30 minutes.

Makes 6 servings.

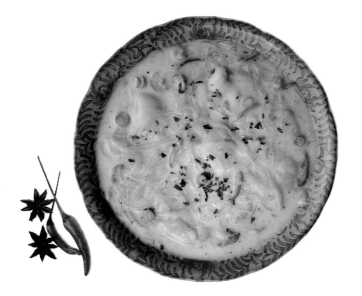

– THAI SHRIMP & NOODLE SOUP –

2 cups fish stock
2 stalks lemon grass, crushed and chopped
2 small star anise pods
2 garlic cloves, chopped
2 cups coconut milk
8 large raw shrimp, shelled
4 shelled scallops, halved horizontally
3 ounces clear vermicelli, soaked in cold water 10
   minutes, then drained
2 green onions, thinly sliced
2 fresh red chiles, seeded and sliced
Juice of 1-1/2 limes
1 tablespoon fish sauce
1 tablespoon chopped fresh cilantro

In a saucepan, bring stock to a boil. Add lemon grass, star anise, and garlic, then simmer, uncovered, 5 minutes. Cover and let stand 30 minutes.

To pan, add coconut milk. Heat to simmering point. Add shrimp and scallops. Poach 1 minute, then add noodles, green onions, and chiles and cook 1 minute longer until shrimp are pink. Remove pan from heat and stir in lime juice, fish sauce, and chopped cilantro.

Makes 4 servings.

—MEDITERRANEAN FISH SOUP—

2-1/2 pounds mixed fish and shellfish, such as
  monkfish, red mullet, bass, bream, snapper, shrimp,
  and mussels
Pinch saffron threads, toasted and crushed
5 tablespoons olive oil
2 Spanish onions, sliced
1 stalk celery, sliced
3 garlic cloves, chopped
3 large tomatoes, peeled
Bouquet garni of 1 bay leaf, sprig each dried thyme and
  fennel, 3 parsley sprigs, and a strip dried orange peel
5-1/2 cups fish stock
Salt and pepper
Torn basil or chopped fresh parsley to garnish
French bread to serve

Skin and fillet fish (see page 10) and cut into
fairly large pieces. Remove shellfish from
their shells. Soak saffron in 2 tablespoons
warm water 10 minutes. In a large saucepan,
heat oil. Add onions, celery, and garlic and
cook gently until softened. Chop tomatoes
and add to pan with bouquet garni. Arrange
fish on vegetables. Add saffron liquid, then
pour in sufficient stock to cover fish. Simmer, uncovered, 6 minutes.

To the pan, add any shellfish and mussels.
Simmer 3 to 4 minutes longer until shellfish
are just tender and mussels open; discard any
mussels that remain closed. Season with salt
and pepper. Serve garnished with basil or
parsley and accompanied by French bread.

Makes 6 servings.

SEAFOOD GUMBO

2 tablespoons olive oil
2 onions, chopped, and 2 garlic cloves, crushed
1 green bell pepper, cored and chopped
1 stalk celery, chopped
2 tablespoons seasoned flour
3 cups fish stock
1 (14-1/2-oz.) can chopped tomatoes
2/3 cup chopped cooked ham
Bouquet garni
8 ounces fresh okra, sliced
8 ounces each white crab meat and cooked shelled
    shrimp
14 ounces firm white fish fillets, cut into chunks
Lemon juice and dash hot-pepper sauce
2-1/2 cups boiled long-grain rice to serve

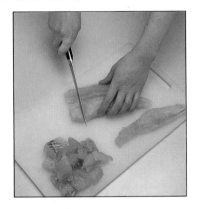

In a heavy flameproof casserole, heat oil. Add onions and cook until softened. Add garlic, bell pepper, and celery and cook, stirring frequently, 5 minutes. Sprinkle flour over and stir 1 minute longer. Stir in stock, tomatoes, ham, and bouquet garni. Partially cover and simmer 30 minutes longer. Add okra and simmer, covered, 30 minutes.

Chop crab meat and shrimp. Add fish to casserole and cook about 7 minutes. Add crab meat and shrimp and cook about 2-1/2 minutes until shrimp are hot. Add lemon juice and hot-pepper sauce to taste. Spoon rice into warm serving bowls and ladle gumbo over it.

Makes 4 to 6 servings.

Note: Sprinkle chopped fresh parsley over the top, if wished.

LOBSTER WITH BASIL DRESSING

4 lobsters, 1 to 1-1/4 pounds, each
Mâche and lemon wedges to serve
DRESSING:
1/3 cup drained and chopped sun-dried tomatoes in
    olive oil
1 small bunch basil, chopped
4 tablespoons walnut oil
2 tablespoons sherry vinegar
Pepper

To make dressing, chop tomatoes and basil together. In a small bowl, beat together oil and vinegar, then stir in tomatoes and basil. Season with black pepper.

Using a large, heavy knife, and working from head to tail along the back, split lobsters in half. Remove and discard intestine that runs through center to tail, stomach from near head, and spongy gills.

Brush cut side of lobsters generously with dressing and set aside 15 minutes. Preheat broiler. Broil lobster about 3 minutes. Meanwhile, gently warm remaining dressing in a small saucepan. Brush lobster with dressing and serve with mâche leaves, and lemon wedges. Serve remaining dressing separately.

Makes 4 servings.

—CRAB & BLACK BEAN SAUCE—

1-1/2 pound fresh whole crab, cooked
1-1/4 tablespoons peanut oil
2 to 3 garlic cloves, crushed
3 whole green onions, cut into 2-inch pieces
3 (1/4-inch) slices fresh gingerroot, chopped
2 tablespoons fermented black beans
2 fresh red chiles, seeded and thinly sliced
1-1/4 tablespoons soy sauce
2 tablespoons rice wine or medium-dry sherry
1/2 cup fish stock, preferably made from shrimp shells
   and heads
Cilantro sprigs to garnish

Detach claws and legs from crab, then divide claws at joints. Using nutcrackers or a sharp, heavy knife, lightly crack claws and legs so as not to damage the flesh inside. Place crab on its back with tail flap toward you. Holding shell, press body section upward from under tail flap and ease out with thumbs. Pull off inedible gray gills and discard. Using the knife, cut crab body into quarters. Using a spoon, remove stomach bag and mouth from back shell. Scrape out brown meat. Heat a wok or large skillet, then add oil.

When it is hot. Add garlic, green onions, and gingerroot and stir-fry until fragrant. Add black beans, chiles, and crab, stir-fry 2 minutes longer, then add soy sauce, rice wine, and stock. Tip contents of wok or skillet into a flameproof, heavy casserole. Cover and cook 5 minutes longer. Serve garnished with cilantro.

Makes 4 servings.

CRAB SOUFFLÉ

3 tablespoons butter
1 tablespoon grated onion
5 tablespoons all-purpose flour
3/4 cup milk
2/3 cup cream cheese
3 tablespoons chopped fresh parsley
1-1/2 teaspoons anchovy extract
2 to 3 teaspoons lemon juice
5 eggs, separated
8 ounces mixed white and brown crab meat
Salt and pepper
1 egg white
2 tablespoons freshly grated Parmesan cheese
Orange and fennel salad to serve
Marjoram sprigs to garnish

Preheat oven to 400F (205C). Put a baking sheet to heat on lowest shelf. Butter a 2-1/2 quart soufflé dish. In a saucepan, melt butter. Add onion and cook 2 to 3 minutes. Stir in flour, cook 1 minute, then gradually stir in milk. Bring to a boil, stirring, then simmer gently 4 minutes, stirring occasionally. Remove pan from heat. Stir in cream cheese, chopped parsley, anchovy extract, lemon juice, egg yolks, and crab. Season with salt and pepper.

Beat egg whites until stiff but not dry. Stir in 2 tablespoons crab mixture, then fold egg whites into remaining crab mixture in 3 batches. Transfer to soufflé dish. Sprinkle Parmesan cheese over top and place dish on baking sheet. Bake 40 to 45 minutes until lightly set in center. Serve immediately with orange and fennel salad, garnished with sprigs of marjoram.

Makes 4 to 6 servings.

CAJUN CRABCAKES

1 small clove garlic, finely chopped
2 tablespoons finely chopped white and green parts of
   green onions
2 tablespoons finely chopped red bell pepper
1 egg, beaten
1-1/2 tablespoons mayonnaise
1 pound fresh white and brown crab meat, chopped
1 tablespoon chopped fresh parsley
2 cups fresh bread crumbs
Squeeze lemon juice
Salt and red (cayenne) pepper
Olive oil for shallow frying
Sour cream and snipped chives and crisp green salad to
   serve

In a mortar or small bowl, put garlic, green onions, bell pepper, and a pinch salt. Crush together using a pestle or end of a rolling pin. Stir in egg, mayonnaise, crab meat, parsley, and about half the bread crumbs to bind together. Add lemon juice, salt, and cayenne to taste.

Form crab mixture into 8 cakes, 3/4 inch thick and 2 1/2 inches round. Lightly press in remaining bread crumbs. Chill 1 hour. In a nonstick skillet, heat a thin layer oil. Add crab cakes in batches and fry 3 to 4 minutes on each side until golden. Serve warm with sour cream and chives, and a crisp green salad.

Makes 8.

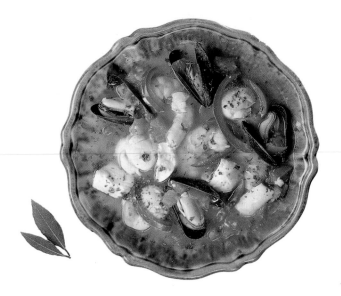

CIOPPINO

2 tablespoons light olive oil
1 large onion, chopped
3 garlic cloves, chopped
1 small red chile, seeded and thinly sliced
1 red bell pepper, seeded and sliced
1 pound tomatoes
1 cup fish stock
1/2 cup dry white wine
1 teaspoon dried oregano
1-1/2 teaspoons each chopped fresh thyme and
     marjoram and 1 bay leaf
8 ounces haddock, cod, or halibut fillet, skinned
8 ounces large raw shrimp
16 mussels, cleaned (see page 11)
4 large scallops, shelled (see page 11)
2-1/2 tablespoons chopped fresh parsley

In a large, heavy saucepan, heat oil. Add onion, garlic, chile, and bell pepper. Cook gently until onion begins to color. Meanwhile, peel, seed, and chop tomatoes. Add to pan with stock, wine, and herbs. Cover and simmer 45 minutes.

Cut fish into cubes and shell shrimp. To pan, add mussels, then simmer 1 minute. Add haddock, shrimp, and scallops. Cook over low heat 3 to 5 minutes until mussels open; discard any that remain closed. Sprinkle with parsley and serve at once.

Makes 4 servings.

Note: Garnish with 8 unshelled, cooked large shrimp, if liked.

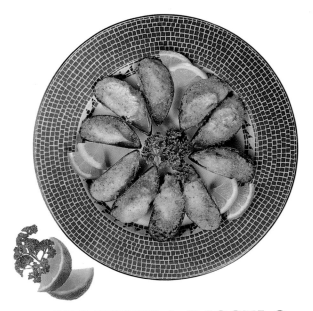

STUFFED MUSSELS

1 shallot, finely chopped
4 sprigs parsley
2 sprigs thyme
1/2 cup dry white wine (optional)
2 pounds mussels, cleaned (see page 11)
Crusty bread to serve
STUFFING:
1 or 2 garlic cloves, halved
4 sprigs parsley
Leaves from 2 sprigs thyme
1 thin slice day-old bread
4 tablespoons unsalted butter
1 teaspoon grated lemon peel
2 teaspoons lemon juice
1-1/4 teaspoons Dijon mustard
Salt and pepper

Into a large saucepan, put shallot, parsley, thyme, and wine or 1/2 cup water. Simmer a few minutes, then add mussels. Cover pan, bring to a boil, and cook mussels 4 to 5 minutes, shaking pan frequently, until shells open; discard any that remain closed. Meanwhile, make stuffing. In a food processor or blender, chop garlic and herbs together. Remove crusts from bread and add bread to food processor or blender with butter, lemon peel and juice, mustard, salt, and pepper; set aside.

Preheat broiler. Discard top shells from mussels. Strain cooking juices and add 2 to 3 teaspoons to stuffing to moisten it. Using a teaspoon, spread a generous amount of stuffing on each mussel, then place in a shallow baking dish. Broil about 3 minutes until golden and bubbling. Serve with plenty of crusty bread.

Makes 2 servings.

Note: Garnish with lemon and lime slices and sprigs of parsley.

— MUSSELS IN TOMATO SAUCE —

2 tablespoons olive oil
2 shallots, finely chopped
2 garlic cloves, crushed
2/3 cup medium-dry white wine
1-1/2 cups peeled, seeded, and chopped tomatoes
Finely grated peel of 1 lemon
2 tablespoons capers, drained and chopped
3 tablespoons chopped fresh parsley
3 pounds fresh mussels, cleaned
Salt and pepper
Crusty bread to serve

In a large saucepan, heat oil. Add shallots and garlic and cook gently until softened. Add wine, tomatoes, lemon peel, capers, and half the parsley. Bring to a boil.

To pan, add mussels. Cover and cook over high heat 3 to 4 minutes, or until mussel shells open, shaking pan frequently; discard any mussels that remain closed. Season with salt and pepper. Transfer to large bowls or soup plates, sprinkle remaining parsley over and serve with crusty bread.

Makes 2 to 3 servings.

INDONESIAN STEAMED MUSSELS

2 pounds mussels or clams, cleaned
1 (3-inch) piece lemon grass, crushed and chopped
1 (3-inch) piece fresh gingerroot, chopped
10 sprigs basil
Torn basil leaves to garnish
SWEET-AND-SOUR SAUCE:
14 ounces red bell peppers, seeded and chopped
2 ounces fresh red chiles, seeded and chopped
3 garlic cloves, roughly chopped
4 tablespoons sugar
6 tablespoons vinegar
2 tablespoons olive oil
Salt

To make sauce, into a blender or food processor, put bell peppers, chiles, garlic, and 2
tablespoons water. Transfer to a non-
aluminum saucepan. Add remaining sauce
ingredients with 2/3 cup water. Bring to a
boil, then simmer 20 minutes or until
reduced by half. Leave to cool, then transfer
to a jar and refrigerate to allow flavors to
develop. (It can be refrigerated up to 2
weeks.)

Into a large saucepan, put clams or mussels,
lemon grass, ginger, and basil sprigs. Add
sufficient water to come 1-1/2 inches up sides
of pan. Bring to a boil, cover, and cook over
medium heat 3 to 5 minutes until shells open;
discard any that remain closed. Meanwhile,
into a small bowl, transfer sauce. Drain
mussels or clams. Garnish with torn basil and
serve with sauce.

Makes 4 servings.

OYSTERS ROCKEFELLER

Kosher salt
24 oysters, opened, on the half shell
1/2 cup butter
2 shallots, finely chopped
1 stalk celery, finely chopped
4-1/2 cups finely chopped spinach
1 tablespoon chopped fresh parsley
1-1/2 teaspoons chopped fresh tarragon
2 tablespoons fresh bread crumbs
1 tablespoon Pernod or pastis
Dash hot-pepper sauce and Worcestershire sauce
Salt and pepper

In a broiler pan, spread a generous layer of kosher salt over bottom. Nestle oysters in salt.

In a saucepan or skillet, melt one-quarter of the butter. Add shallots and celery and cook gently until softened but not colored. Stir in spinach, parsley, and tarragon. Cook over medium heat until surplus moisture from spinach evaporates.

Preheat broiler. In a blender or food processor, puree spinach mixture. Mix in bread crumbs, remaining butter, Pernod or pastis, and hot-pepper and Worcestershire sauces. Season with salt and pepper. Place tablespoonful of spinach mixture on each oyster. Broil about 3 minutes until beginning to turn golden. Serve at once.

Makes 4 servings.

Note: Garnish with lemon slices and sprigs of parsley, if wished.

ANGELS ON HORSEBACK

4 slices bacon
8 oysters, shelled
4 slices bread
Unsalted butter for spreading
Pepper
Mâche and lemon twists to garnish

Preheat broiler. Cut each bacon slice across in half, then stretch each piece with the back of a knife. Wrap a piece of bacon around each oyster, then place on a broiler tray with ends of bacon underneath.

Toast bread. Broil oysters until crisp, then turn over and crisp the other side.

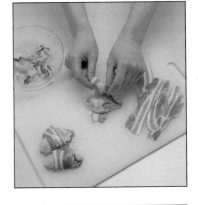

Meanwhile, cut 2 circles from each slice of toast, then butter circles. Place one oyster on each circle. Grind black pepper over and serve garnished with mâche and lemon twists.

Makes 8.

OYSTERS IN COFFINS

2 miniature brioches
1/4 cup unsalted butter, melted
6 large oysters
4 tablespoons sour cream
Red (cayenne) pepper and white pepper
Finely grated lemon peel and slices to garnish
Tomato, onion, and tarragon salad to serve

Preheat oven to 425F (220C). Remove top knobs from brioches. Scoop out insides to leave a thin shell, taking care not to pierce walls. Brush brioches inside and out with half the melted butter. On a baking sheet, place hollowed-out brioches. Bake 5 to 10 minutes until crisp.

Meanwhile, scrub oysters. To open, holding one at a time in a cloth, curved side down, prize open shells at hinge using a strong, short-bladed knife. Loosen each oyster. Into a saucepan, pour liquid with remaining melted butter. Boil a few minutes until liquid is reduced, then, over low heat, stir in sour cream. Heat gently without boiling. Season with cayenne and white peppers.

In each brioche, place 3 oysters. Pour sauce over oysters. Garnish with lemon peel and slices and serve with tomato, onion, and tarragon salad.

Makes 2 servings.

KEDGEREE

1-1/4 pounds smoked haddock or salmon
1/2 cup long-grain rice
2 tablespoons lemon juice
2/3 cup light or sour cream
Pinch freshly grated nutmeg
Red (cayenne) pepper
2 hard-cooked eggs, shelled and chopped
4 tablespoons butter, diced
2 tablespoons chopped fresh parsley
Parsley sprigs and sliced hard-cooked eggs to garnish

In a large skillet that will take fish in a single layer, poach fish just covered by water about 10 minutes. Lift fish from cooking liquid and discard bones and skin. Flake flesh. Measure fish cooking liquid to twice volume of rice; top up with water if necessary. Into a saucepan, put liquid and rice. Bring to a boil. Add rice, and stir, then cover and simmer about 15 minutes until rice is tender and liquid absorbed. Meanwhile, preheat oven to 350F (175C). Butter a baking dish.

Remove rice from heat. Stir in lemon juice, cream, fish, nutmeg, and a pinch of cayenne. Gently fold in eggs. In an openproof serving dish, put rice mixture. Dot with butter and bake about 25 minutes. Stir chopped parsley into kedgeree and garnish with parsley sprigs and sliced hard-cooked egg. Sprinkle a little cayenne over top, if wished.

Makes 4 servings.

-HADDOCK IN BAKED POTATOES-

4 large baking potatoes, scrubbed and pricked
   with a fork
1 pound smoked haddock
1 cup milk
2 to 3 teaspoons lemon juice
Pepper
5 to 6 tablespoons sour cream or plain yogurt
2 tablespoons snipped fresh chives
1 tablespoon chopped fresh parsley
Salad to serve

Preheat oven to 400F (205C). Bake potatoes
1-1/2 hours until tender.

Meanwhile, into a baking dish, put fish. Pour
milk over, cover with parchment paper or
foil, and cook on bottom shelf in oven about
8 minutes until flesh flakes. Drain fish,
reserving milk. Flake flesh finely, discarding
skin and bones. Season with lemon juice and
pepper. In a small bowl, mix together sour
cream or yogurt, chives, parsley, and pepper
to taste.

Cut a slice from top of each potato. Scoop out
most of insides of potatoes, taking care not to
pierce skins. Into a bowl, place potato flesh.
Beat potato with reserved milk and pepper to
taste, then mix in the flaked fish. Spoon fish
mixture back into potato skins. Spoon half
the sour cream or yogurt mixture over the
top. Return to oven about 10 minutes. Pour
remaining cream or yogurt over. Serve with
salad.

Makes 4 servings.

—OMELET ARNOLD BENNETT—

6 ounces smoked haddock fillet, poached and flaked
4 tablespoons butter, diced
3/4 cup whipping cream
4 eggs, separated
Pepper
1/2 cup shredded aged Cheddar cheese
Mâche, cress and lemon wedges to garnish

Discard skin and bones from fish and flake flesh. In a fairly small, nonstick saucepan, melt half the butter with 1/4 cup of the cream. Lightly stir in fish. Cover, remove from heat, and let cool.

In a bowl, stir together egg yolks, 1 tablespoon cream, and pepper to taste. Lightly stir in fish mixture. In another bowl, stir together cheese and remaining cream.

Preheat broiler. Beat egg whites until stiff but not dry. Using a large, metal spoon, lightly fold egg white into fish mixture in 3 batches. In an omelet pan, melt remaining butter. Pour in fish mixture and cook until set and lightly browned underneath, but still quite moist on the top. Pour cheese mixture over omelet, then broil until golden and bubbling. Serve garnished with Mâche, cress and lemon wedges.

Makes 2 servings.

—SMOKED SALMON SCRAMBLE—

4 ounces smoked salmon trimmings, chopped
2 tablespoons light cream
3 tablespoons unsalted butter
4 large eggs, beaten
Black pepper
Snipped fresh chives and lime slices to garnish
Buttered toasted bagels or English muffins to serve

In a small bowl, mix together smoked salmon and cream. Leave to stand 10 to 15 minutes.

In a saucepan, melt half the butter. Stir in eggs. Cook over low heat, stirring with a wooden spoon, until beginning to set. Add salmon and cream and season with pepper. Continue to stir until eggs are almost set.

Remove pan from heat and immediately stir in remaining butter. Garnish with snipped chives and lime slices and serve with buttered toasted bagels or English muffins.

Makes 2 servings.

SALMON MILLE FEUILLES

3/4 cup plain yogurt, chilled
3/4 teaspoon chopped dill
Salt and pepper
8 sheets phyllo pastry dough
Melted butter
4 ounces smoked salmon trimmings, ground
2 tablespoons heavy cream, well chilled
1 bunch chives, roughly snipped
12 large slices smoked salmon
Dill sprigs to garnish
Lemon wedges to serve

In a bowl, mix together half of the yogurt, the dill, salt, and pepper. Cover and chill. Preheat oven to 425F (220C). Cut twenty-four 3-inch circles from phyllo pastry. Lay half the circles on a baking sheet, brush with melted butter, then cover each circle with another. Brush with melted butter and bake 5 minutes until golden. Transfer to a wire rack to cool. Into a blender or food processor, put salmon trimmings. With motor running, slowly pour in cream and remaining yogurt until just evenly mixed. Add chives and pepper to taste.

Cut salmon into twelve 3-inch circles. Place pastry circle on a plate, spread with one twelfth of the smoked salmon cream, then cover with a smoked salmon circle. Repeat twice more to make one mille feuille. Make 3 more mille feuille in the same way. Chill. Serve garnished with dill sprigs and accompanied by sauce and lemon wedges.

Makes 4 servings.

INDEX